W9-CTH-364

BONE TO PICK

BONE TO PICK

Of Forgiveness, Reconciliation,

Reparation, and Revenge

ELLIS COSE

ATRIA BOOKS
NEW YORK   LONDON   TORONTO   SYDNEY

ATRIA BOOKS
1230 Avenue of the Americas
New York, NY 10020

Copyright © 2004 by Ellis Cose

Library of Congress Cataloging-in-Publication-Data

Cose, Ellis
    Bone to pick : of forgiveness, reconciliation, reparation, and revenge / Ellis Cose.
       p. cm.
    Includes index.
    ISBN 0-7434-7066-4
       1. Forgiveness. 2. Reconciliation. I. Title

BJ1476.C67 2004
158.2—dc22   2003062983

First Atria Books hardcover printing April 2004

10 9 8 7 6 5 4 3 2 1

ATRIA BOOKS is a trademark of Simon & Schuster, Inc.

Designed by Dana Sloan

Manufactured in the United States of America

For information regarding special discounts for bulk purchases,
please contact Simon & Schuster Special Sales at 1-800-456-6798
or business@simonandschuster.com

For Elisa Maria

CONTENTS

ACKNOWLEDGMENTS

RARELY HAS AN AUTHOR RECEIVED ASSIS-
tance from so many hearts and minds as have I in writing this
book. Judith Curr, my publisher, and Malaika Adero, my editor,
believed in *Bone to Pick* when it was little more than a notion.
Their confidence and support brought it into the world. I am also
heavily indebted to Michael Congdon, my longtime agent, sound-
ing board and honest critic, without whose efforts this book
would not exist.

My colleagues at *Newsweek*, particularly Mark Whitaker, Rick
Smith, Jon Meacham, Marcus Mabry, and Tom Watson, provided
an environment that was always supportive of intellectual
inquiry. The Ford Foundation funded much of the research and
travel, thanks in large measure to the efforts of Anthony Romero,
Alan Jenkins, and Mary McClymont. I will be forever grateful for
their support and also for their understanding as the book evolved
in directions not originally foreseen.

Eduardo González-Cueva, with the Truth and Reconciliation
Commission in Peru, was an invaluable guide and resource. Jerry
Eddings was a wise advisor in South Africa. Dr. Ken A. Attafuah,
executive director of Ghana's National Reconciliation Commission,
and Franklin Oduro, of the Center for Democratic Development,
ensured that my time in Ghana was well spent. Rezaul Karim,

head of CARE in East Timor, supplied advice, logistical support, hospitality, and insightful conversation. Matt Hakiaha gave me a warm Maōri welcome to New Zealand and provided entrée into circles I would never have discovered on my own.

Priscilla Hayner, Lisa Magarrell, Eric Darko, and Ian Martin of the International Center for Transitional Justice were valuable sources of contacts and information. John Sage, founder of Bridges to Life, was both an inspiration and an important resource. Robin Brinn, of the Jewish Board of Family and Children's Services, generously shared her insights in the area of mental health. Carolyn Boyes-Watson tutored me in peace-making circles and restorative justice.

I thank Oliver Cromwell and Youtha Hardman-Cromwell for convincing me to get on a plane to New Zealand. And I offer my profound appreciation to Lee Llambelis, partner, wife, chief fan, and critic, whose observations were never less than profound and whose faith was a constant source of sustenance.

Finally, I thank the scores of people named and unnamed who invited me into their lives and who shared with me their stories and their wisdom—along with their triumphs and their pain. Without them *Bone to Pick* would have remained a skeleton of an idea with neither flesh nor a soul.

Before traveling to East Timor, I sought out Sergio Vieira de Mello, the former United Nations Special Representative for the Secretary General in East Timor. De Mello had just been promoted to the job of UN High Commissioner for Human Rights and had a great deal to say about the challenges of his new job. He also had much say about the Timorese, and about their caring and forgiving nature. In the course of our conversation, he told a story.

"In March 2000, we brought, for the first time, a group of three militia commanders from West Timor. Two of them were from Baucao. . . . And one was from Los Palos. . . . These were people with blood of their hands, *bastards,* particularly the one from Los

Palos, a true thug. . . . We had prepared the visit. We had informed the population. We had explained why it was important that he come back, because he had told us that he wanted to apologize, to talk to the population of Los Palos and express regret, apologize, and request pardon. . . . But we were rather worried; because in a normal situation in any other country, that guy would have been lynched. He would have been stoned to death. . . . But not only was he not lynched; he came, he addressed the population. . . . And people, rather than cursing him, insulting him, or beating him up, they cried. Normal, simple, humble people cried."

De Mello was making a point not just about East Timor but about the possibility of transformation and reconciliation. Several months later, in August 2003, he was killed when a truck bomb exploded at the UN complex in Baghdad. His loss (and the loss of his colleagues) was a tragedy in every sense of the word; and his death underscored the need for grace and goodwill in the world. I thank him for his wisdom, for his example, and for his faith—a faith that, in Iraq, was so sadly betrayed.

INTRODUCTION

HONORING THE PAST, HEALING THE SOUL

CHOOSE LIFE GOES A POPULAR SAYING, expressing a sentiment that is undeniably noble and good. Yet in fact, we have little choice in the matter. For life is a gift—one that chooses us. Our decision is in what we do with that life, with how we endeavor to lead it—with how tenaciously, and wisely, we defend it; with how well we cope with its tragedies and hardships.

In the course of researching this book, I listened to countless personal narratives, many of them either heartrending or shocking, a fair number of them inspirational. Perhaps the most powerful was the story shared with me by a poor peasant woman from a tiny village in Peru.

She was snatched from her home for no apparent reason. Then she was shot in the back of the head at point-blank range and tossed into a river and left for dead. Somehow she survived. And she managed to get on with her life.

Her ordeal (and I will tell her story in more detail later) was unimaginably horrific—infinitely more so than anything most of us are ever likely to go through. Yet, in a sense, her challenge is

1

one we have all faced—albeit on a markedly lesser scale. For we have all been unjustly harmed. And somehow we manage to deal with it.

Much of living, as we all learn, is about dealing with pain caused by others, about accepting the pain or getting past it, about reconciling with—or trying to move beyond the reach of—those who caused it. The child eventually accepts the loss of a parent; a parent even accepts the loss of a child. And in time a people, individually and collectively, fashion lives no longer quite so focused on the horrors of apartheid, the genocide of Rwanda, the hell of the Holocaust, the mass murder of Armenians, or the devastation of September 11.

Yet to deal with pain or trauma, to "get over it," is not the same as being free of it. An abusive lover may get so deep under your skin that you find it nearly impossible to let go. An unforeseen tragedy may so shake your faith that years later you curse the capriciousness of fate. Or question the goodness of God. Injuries take on a life of their own. So even when the wound seems all but healed, the pain and the memories linger—sometimes for days, sometimes for months, sometimes for generations.

Psychologist Robert Enright found that nearly half of a group of over two hundred seven-year-olds he worked with in Northern Ireland were clinically depressed. The reason, he speculated, had a lot to do with the centuries of suffering the people of Northern Ireland have endured. Somehow the parents transmitted their trauma to their children. "When husbands and wives marry," observed Enright, "they bring what they learned from their mom and dad. . . . They bring in the wounds of the earlier generation, which also brought in the wounds of the earlier generation." At a 1997 conference on Northern Ireland at Georgetown University, political scientist Paul Arthur made much the same point. "This sense of memory, I think, has been one of our deadliest problems."

This is a book about memory and a book about wounds. About the honoring of one; about the healing of the other. It is about the complex—sometimes insidious—relationship between the two; and about the movement—actually many movements—flowering at the intersection. It is about memory recovered and memory denied, about making amends and also excuses; and about the search for relief from wounds that won't heal unless swaddled in the gift of forgiveness.

This is not to say that forgiveness and reconciliation are always possible. Brutes, bullies, and people beyond redemption will always have a place in the world. Rogue states are, by definition, beyond civilized constraints. And at times they must be met with something significantly more compelling than an understanding heart. The need for justice, the call to war, the hunger for revenge: all are as old as mankind, and no less enduring.

As I write this, American troops are in Iraq. A proposal for a truth-and-reconciliation commission is on the table, but no one expects one to be formed anytime soon. Not even the strongest proponents of national reconciliation believe a commission alone could heal the wounds—both new and old—from which that country suffers. Yet only a simpleton would suggest that Iraq's future can be divorced from the memory of its past or that its wounds can be left untended without consequence.

Upon accepting the Nobel Prize for literature in 1980 Czeslaw Milosz declared, "It is possible that there is no other memory than the memory of wounds." Surely no other memories are more powerful, more corrosive, or more enduring. And lately those memories have sent a new generation in unlikely directions. They have impelled crime victims from Austin to Australia to commune with perpetrators, spawned truth commissions around the world, and sired a branch of psychology anchored in the conviction that forgiveness is the key to inner peace—and man's best hope for ending trauma that has lasted for generations.

In the following pages, we will focus less on the deadly consequences of memory than on its converse: the harm that comes from not giving memory its due. We will meet people from South

Africa, to East Timor, to Greensboro, North Carolina, who see sifting through painful memories—exposing ugliness to light—as a sacred duty and as the key to their people's salvation. Herein also are parables of forgiveness and reconciliation; stories of extraordinary individuals who have learned a powerful lesson: that moving from trauma to recovery, from tragedy to renewal, sometimes means reaching out to those you have every right to hate.

There are those people—the few, the special—who come to such attitudes and behavior naturally. They seem to float through the world, free of rancor, on a cloud of charity and goodwill. When I asked John Lewis, the congressman from Georgia, how— in his life as a grassroots civil rights leader—he had avoided anger while being beaten, repeatedly, by cops in the Jim Crow South, he answered like the seminary graduate he is: "If you believe there is a spark of the divine in every human being . . . you cannot get to the point where you hate that person, or despise that person . . . even if that person beats you. . . . You have to have the capacity, the ability to forgive."

Few of us glimpse the divine in bullwhip-wielding bullies. Or see much point in forgiving sadism—even if sanctioned by the state. But what if the spirit of mercy can be taught—or at least actively nurtured? Are there any benefits other than knowing that God has touched one's soul? Richard Nethercut's experience argues that there can be, not just for the world—which can only gain if vindictiveness wanes—but also for the victimized individual seeking peace.

A thin, angular man in his seventies with dark, mostly receded hair and a gentle, earnest manner, Nethercut spends much of his time these days working with prisoners. It was a path he could not have foreseen while growing up in Wisconsin during the 1930s. After serving two years in the army during World War II, he earned a master's degree from the Fletcher School of Law and Diplomacy at Tufts University, and eventually ended up in Hong Kong, as a foreign service officer. In Shanghai in 1960, Nethercut and his wife, Lorraine, adopted a two-year-old girl of Russian descent.

Eight years later, Nethercut was assigned to the State Department's Washington headquarters. Their daughter, Eugenia—or Jaina, as they called her—had trouble adjusting to America. Nonetheless, she made it through high school and decided to go to Washington State University. But instead of focusing on her studies, Jaina began hanging out with a sleazy crowd. And in January 1978, she ended up in a welfare hotel in Seattle, apparently looking for marijuana.

She went to the room of a man she reportedly had met the previous night. The man, stoned out of his head, attacked her. She struggled. She managed to get out of the door; but she was dragged back in, raped, and strangled with a pair of stockings. It was Martin Luther King Jr.'s birthday. Jaina was nineteen years old.

The news left Nethercut angry, shocked, and struggling with feelings of powerlessness. He also felt a great deal of guilt. For Jaina's move out west seemed, at least in part, an attempt to distance herself from her family. She wasn't even using the family name, which, for Nethercut, was a source of shame.

Police captured the assailant immediately. And though Nethercut couldn't bear to go to the trial, he was happy the man was sentenced to life in prison. Still, Nethercut was unable to put the tragedy behind him. He was depressed, and his State Department career seemed stalled. Though only in his midfifties, he took early retirement two years after Jaina's death and moved to Concord, his wife's hometown, the place where his daughter was buried.

Shortly after the move, Nethercut felt an inexplicable desire to contact the man who had murdered his daughter. He wrote to the chaplain at the Washington State Penitentiary in Walla Walla, Washington. Weeks later the chaplain called as the murderer waited to get on the line. The conversation lasted roughly ten minutes. Nethercut scarcely remembers what was said. He does recall that the conversation was awkward. "We both danced around the issue. We were quite polite with each other. I wanted to learn more and I didn't learn more. . . . I couldn't understand what had happened." The man expressed regret and yet never acknowledged his crime, and certainly didn't provide the explanation and apology Nethercut so desperately craved. Nevertheless, Nethercut muttered words—insincere though they were—of forgiveness.

The men exchanged Christmas cards a few times; but there was no real relationship to maintain—and no release from the confusion and impotence Nethercut felt. For years, he bottled up his emotions: "I kept my daughter's death to myself. I suppressed it. I didn't go through an authentic grieving process." He blamed himself for being a bad father and wallowed in anger and guilt. Finally, he got psychiatric help for his depression; and he got more involved in the activities of his Congregationalist church.

At a religious retreat in 1986 Nethercut had an encounter that radically changed his life. A Catholic bishop suggested that he become part of a prison Bible fellowship program. The idea strongly appealed to Nethercut, who was searching for a way to fill "the hole in my soul . . . I really wanted to do something positive." Several years later, he got involved in the Alternatives to Violence Program, a two-and-a-half-day immersion experience that brings together prisoners and outsiders to role-play, confess, confide, empathize, and explore ideas about the causes—and cures—for violence. In one of those sessions Nethercut got a chance to role-play the part of the man who had murdered Jaina.

In the exercise, he went before the pretend parole board to make his case for freedom; and for the first time, he felt he understood some part of the man who had killed his daughter. It was unexpectedly empowering.

In 2001, at a national conference of the Alternatives to Violence Program, Nethercut met another man who had murdered a woman. That man, who was no longer in prison, had reached out to the family of the women he had killed; and the family had refused his apology. As the killer and Nethercut talked of their respective experiences, they realized they could help each other. Shortly thereafter they went through a ceremony with a victim-offender mediator. His new friend apologized for the murder and Nethercut accepted. The ritual served its purpose: "I no longer feel the need to hear directly from the man himself."

Nethercut's life has come to revolve around his volunteer work in prison—and in promoting prison reform and nonviolence. It is his way of honoring his daughter, of "giving a gift of significance to my daughter's life." He sees in many of the young prisoners and ex-offenders something of his daughter. "They are angry, alienated, at the same time . . . looking for love, acceptance." And he has come to realize, he says, voicing John Lewis's precise words, that everyone has "a spark of the divine."

Thoughts of the murderer—given parole after seventeen years despite his life sentence—no longer torment Nethercut, who has finally and totally forgiven the man. "Forgiveness is something you do for yourself," said Nethercut. "It releases you from a prison of your own making. You forgive the individual and move on. . . . Reconciliation is a step further. . . . That takes both sides."

Nethercut feels that he is a man transformed, and he is no longer depressed. "I feel more whole, more kind of at peace." Through his work, his faith, determination, and grace, he has turned a tragedy in his past into something about which he feels unequivocally positive.

Nethercut is a very unusual man, one whose spirituality paved the way for his particular journey. But, increasingly, psychologists such as Robert Enright argue that the process of forgiveness can be and should be taught, that it can lead one out of the desert of resentment and rage, that it can be a key to coping with the pain of traumas nursed for years or even generations. I will explore that notion shortly. But let us begin with an idea more modest, yet still grand: that goodwill and confession—acknowledging the sins of the past—can heal a wounded soul, even a wounded nation. That was a large part of the theory behind South Africa's Truth and Reconciliation Commission. The TRC fueled the dream that, by going through a process combining acknowledgment and absolution, a country sundered by years of separatism and violence could move toward genuine reconciliation.

Like countless others who have spent time in South Africa, I was captivated by the dream. The dream's essence was captured by a poster hanging in a tenth-floor hearing room of the Cape Town headquarters of the TRC. *Don't Let Our Nightmares Become Our Children's* read the yellow letters on a black background. *Let's speak out to each other by telling the truth, by telling the stories of the past, so that we can walk the road to reconciliation together* implored smaller white characters beneath.

The commission called on apartheid-era perpetrators of every political stripe to confess their sins in exchange for amnesty from prosecution. Victims also were urged to tell their stories. In return they presumably would find release, closure, and if Parliament cooperated, some modest financial reparation.

By at least one standard the hearings were an astounding success. They exposed some of the deepest secrets of the apartheid state—things whispered about, long suspected, but never before openly admitted. Assassinations, bombings, massacres, mutilation—all were dutifully confessed, along with schemes as bizarre as anything dreamed up by Hitler's henchmen. A covert chemical-biological warfare program contemplated mass sterilization of the black majority through secretly administered drugs. Another scheme envisioned flooding black townships with lethal micro-organisms and hallucinogens. Yet others called for applying deadly poison to clothing worn by student activists and contaminating drinking water with noxious bacteria. The hearings revealed numerous such mad plots. They also created moments of high human drama. At times victim and perpetrator weepingly embraced, bringing tears to the eyes of those in the audience—moving even some of the most cynical to marvel at the human capacity for empathy and conciliation.

Nobel Peace Prize winner and Anglican Archbishop Desmond Tutu chaired the TRC. Along with a *Newsweek* colleague, Marcus Mabry, I interviewed him in his Cape Town office in 1998. The chemical warfare revelations were very much in the news. But it was clear even then that, in some quarters, the TRC was shaping up as something of a disappointment. Victims and victim advocates were already complaining about the lack of reparations and about their inability, in many cases, to get to the truth. Many perpetrators, they said, were lying; and TRC investigators simply didn't have the resources to verify more than a fraction of what they were told. Over the years, those complaints would grow louder.

Tutu acknowledged the imbalance in a process that almost immediately awarded amnesty to perpetrators but made victims wait indefinitely. Only after the wheels of Parliament's bureaucracy had turned would they know whether they would get any compensation. Still, Tutu seemed almost giddy with delight as he described a recent visit to a church.

"It's a very fashionable church in the Afrikaans community," he said. "And I preached and made reference to what we had heard from the chemical and biological warfare programs. . . . One of the six ministers of that church then came up into the pulpit where I was standing and he was in tears because he said he had been an ordained minister for over thirty years and also been chaplain of the defense force and he had not known about these things. What he really wanted to say was 'Can you forgive us?' . . . And as I was sitting down, the congregation gave me a standing ovation. And a few of them also were crying."

Tutu clearly saw the moment as a breakthrough for that group of whites. A dam of psychological innocence had come tumbling down. No longer could they say their hands were totally clean; for the system they had believed in, the leaders they had supported, had shed too much innocent blood.

He talked at length about the contortions people went through to avoid facing the truth. "If a revelation is made about how ghastly you are, or how ghastly the policy has been, which you supported, and which your church said you should support, which basically the whole structures of society was saying, 'These are the policies to support, and we have provided you with considerable privilege . . . in accordance with God's will' . . . and then suddenly you are shown that it is actually evil, I don't know that you would be dancing in the streets in acknowledgment. . . . You would look at all sorts of justifications." Such reactions, Tutu added, were as old as man himself: "When God said to Adam, 'You've broken my law,' Adam didn't say, 'Yes, I did.' He said, 'No . . . It's this woman here.' And when God asked the woman, she said, 'It's the snake.'"

"We are the Children of Adam and Eve," he said solemnly. "Some people have made a study of how human beings deal with an unpleasant truth, like a bereavement, or like you are told you have cancer. You deny, you're angry, you make bargains. And, if you are fortunate, you eventually move to the point of acceptance." Coming from Tutu, who had recently been diagnosed with prostate cancer, the point was particularly poignant.

South Africa's Truth and Reconciliation Commission was not the first such body convened. Sixteen so-called truth commissions came before it, according to a count by Priscilla Hayner, author of *Unspeakable Truths*. Uganda, Argentina, Nepal, Germany, and a number of other countries had experimented with the process. Indeed, two of the truth commissions had been in South Africa— appointed by the African National Congress to investigate its own alleged abuses of prisoners and detainees. But though Archbishop Tutu's TRC was not the first, it was far and away the most popular. And because it was so celebrated, it inspired numerous others in places as disparate as Peru and East Timor.

Each commission has had its unique approach to two key questions: *How do you most effectively and most compassionately conduct the search for truth? How do you help a nation and suffering individuals to put the past behind?* In some countries the process has been as simple as granting a blanket or provisional amnesty. In others it involves seeking and accepting an apology for past deeds. In yet others, it means helping people determine what became of their loved one, where—in a literal sense—the bodies were buried. Many victims, of course, are seeking answers to even more difficult questions, questions having to do with the origins of evil. *What drove people to do such awful things? And, having done them, were the perpetrators truly capable of remorse?*

Several years ago, over lunch in a fashionable Cape Town restaurant, Alex Boraine, deputy chairperson of South Africa's TRC, spoke of the difficulties inherent in the TRC's mandate. "I think some people expected there to be even more truth than we have been able to lay our hands on. I think they imagined that the process would be a lot less complicated than it has been. . . . We had sixty-odd trained investigators. That's all we could afford. . . . We could have done with two hundred. We were sidetracked, quite deliberately, by people who made it very difficult. . . . A lot of records were destroyed, deliberately so."

But he, like Tutu, felt that in the end the TRC had performed a great service, that it had opened the eyes of people, even such as himself, who thought they were beyond surprise. "I thought I knew my country. I really thought I knew the extent of its racial policies. My whole life has been fighting, however modestly or ineffectually, against it. And I never, never knew that torture . . . was not confined to certain key prisons, but was endemic throughout the country. It's not a police station in the country where it wasn't practiced as a way of life. And that's come as a hell of a shock. And the realization of just how vicious the system has been. . . . I didn't realize really the amount of suffering that has taken place in this country, just how deep in the psyche of the nation this has been, and therefore, of course, how much work has to be done over a long period of time to restore this."

Something else surprised him: "The generosity of spirit of so many people who have been hurt so badly. . . . They have said, 'We are sick and tired of people going to prison . . . I just want to know what happened, and who did it and why.' The possibility of forgiveness is there."

Thandi Shezi is the living embodiment of that possibility. We met in May 2002 in her tiny office in Johannesburg within the headquarters of the Khulumani Support Group—an organization born after the end of apartheid to help those who suffered at the hands of apartheid's enforcers. She is a short, round—though not quite fat—woman of early middle age with deep brown skin, tight thin braids, and a sweet, shy smile that tends to come out when she relates a memory that is particularly distressing. The smile showed itself quite a lot the morning we talked.

She grew up in Soweto, the most famous of South Africa's black townships. For as long as she can remember, she had chafed under apartheid, at being treated with so much less respect than whites, at watching her mother and other family members work around the clock for pennies, at being forced to study math and other subjects in the tongue of the oppressor. She was part of the fed-up generation, the generation that collectively shouted "no more"; the generation that took to the streets in mass protest against the using of the Afrikaans language in teaching in 1976. Nearly seven hundred people died in that protest, most of them shot by the police. Barely in her teens at the time, Shezi joined the protestors. She was relatively lucky. Though she was shot with a rubber bullet, she survived, along with the scar she still carries on her left leg.

Given her resentment and the historical moment in which she came of age, it was inevitable that Shezi would end up working— albeit at a lowly, clerical level—for a community organization fighting against apartheid.

That work led to her arrest in 1988. The police poured out of perhaps twenty cars and swept her up with several others during a search, they claimed, for ammunition. "As they took me from home, I was beaten with the butt of guns. They kicked me." The handcuffs were so tight that she still bears the scars. And the handcuffs, she discovered, were to be the least of her worries.

It was their intention to break her, to force her to talk by destroying any sense she might have of her own power or dignity. They began by forcing her to watch their assault of a friend, a man with whom she had worked, who was pushed up against a desk with his penis dangling within an open drawer. Unless she talked, they told her, they would slam the drawer. She cried out in protest, begging them to accept the fact that she knew nothing; but they ignored her cries and delivered on their threat—provoking a scream so chilling, so unbearably heartrending, that she can hear it still. "While he's screaming they come to me and said, 'You want to tell us anything?' And I said, 'I know nothing.' "

Later, when they had finished with her friend, they turned their total attention to her. They took her into a room and beat her. Four different white policemen raped her, leaving her a bloody mess and her dress ripped to shreds. "When I came in I was swollen . . . I couldn't even walk properly. . . . Can you imagine your hands being in cuffs and four men raping you without any defense, and you can't talk properly because your whole body is in pain?"

They covered her head with a sack that was wet down with water. The wet bag treatment was a well-developed torture technique. As she breathed in, the wet sack would cling to her nostrils, taking her to the edge of suffocation. And then they applied the electric shocks, which, among other things, forced her teeth to clamp repeatedly on her tongue as her mouth, pressed tightly against the bag, fought to suck in air.

Eventually, they took her to a doctor. She was barely able to walk and unable to talk. "And because I couldn't talk—my tongue was so swollen—they told the doctor that I was a prostitute, that I was trying to escape when I bit my tongue." She stood by, suffering and seething, unable to tell the truth.

She was incarcerated in solitary confinement for roughly a year and never tried for any crime. And when she finally emerged, she kept the horrors to herself, not even sharing with her mother the details of her journey through hell. Instead, she expressed her anger by lashing out—sometimes violently—at her family and her friends.

It was her work with Khulumani that led her to open up. When the TRC began taking testimony in 1996, the organization encouraged its clients to get involved, to seize the opportunity to tell what they knew and to get some measure of compensation for what they had endured. Shezi was hostile to the idea. She was totally opposed to the concept of amnesty for perpetrators. She also doubted that testifying would give her much solace. "I didn't want to go and open up my wounds. At the end of the day I would go home with a hungry stomach, with the kids not going to school. . . . What was the use for me of going to the TRC to submit?" What kind of satisfaction was possible for one who had been through such horrors?

Her colleagues eventually persuaded her she had to testify, that it would be hypocritical to urge others who came to Khulumani to go before the TRC if she was not willing to do so herself. So she filed her statement. When she was selected in 1998 to give public testimony with other women who had been abused, she persuaded herself that the experience would be healing.

"To me, it was like opening up my wounds and giving me a chance to tell the whole world actually what was happening behind closed doors in detention. And also it was for me to say how brutal was the apartheid system when it comes to women. . . . Actually, it was a sense of relief. At last I told somebody about my pain. At last, I opened up."

There were also some ugly consequences. As a result of the

public and heavily covered hearing, her daughter and son, fifteen
and thirteen respectively, were teased about their mom having
been raped. The experience was so difficult for them that she
arranged counseling at a trauma center.

But it was the second part of the TRC procedure—the part
where perpetrators came forward to tell their stories in exchange
for amnesty—that tore her apart. She came expecting some sense
of closure but instead ran into a wall of denial. One of those white
cops who had brutalized her—whose face was branded on her
memory—refused to admit knowing her at all or participating in
the acts that she described. So she sat stunned, listening to him in
horror. Her imagination had conjured up a totally different scene,
one in which he would acknowledge what he had done and she
could accept his remorse. Instead "he's totally denying everything. . . . That was my chance to tell him 'Everything that you and
your friends did to me, I forgive you.' But I couldn't say that
because he was saying 'I don't know you. I haven't seen you.' And I
said, 'You are the one who suggested that black policeman should
put a sack over my head. You are the one.' He said, 'No, I don't
remember.' . . . I felt like I was empty."

Thus the scars of the so-called reconciliation process were
added to the scars apartheid had left on her leg and wrists. And
the one tangible thing she had been promised, monetary reparations for her suffering, had yet to be delivered in any meaningful
amount.

A decade and a half after her arrest and torture, she was still
living with the pain of memories, the pain from lack of acknowledgment that real reparations would represent. And she was tormented by the idea that people who committed awful abuses were
walking around free in the townships; that others who danced
around the truth have held on to their nice positions and houses;
and she wondered whether the reconciliation process, so widely
celebrated, was designed more for perpetrators than victims.

"There is no reconciliation without the truth," she concluded.

"And there is no reconciliation without reparations. Yes, it's reconciled the top guns of the government, because now they are sitting high and they are earning a good salary. But the grassroots people are not reconciled; because if I say, 'I reconciled with my perpetrator and my perpetrator is now a station commander and is earning fifty thousand rands a month and I'm living in a shack,' can you call that reconciliation? No it's not reconciliation. . . . I managed to reconcile with what happened to me. But I haven't reconciled with the perpetrators because I didn't get any truth. I didn't get anything out of it."

Shezi's story is not so unusual in South Africa; nor is it exactly typical. Everyone's story has its own lessons and truths. But both Shezi's and Nethercut's experiences demonstrate how difficult it can be to shake free of the wounds of the past even when the victimized party is willing; they demonstrate as well how difficult the search for common ground can be, how bringing victim and perpetrators together doesn't necessarily lead to confession or catharsis but sometimes simply deepens the pain.

Nonetheless, in talking to both Shezi and Nethercut, I was deeply moved by their shared compulsion to forgive. In both cases that impulse is rooted, to some substantial degree, in their respective views of the role of a good Christian. But it seemed rooted, as well, in the need to believe in the possibility—to use Alex Boraine's term—of "restoration of the moral order."

When that order is shaken—by murder, by torture, by simple betrayal—individuals are understandably thrown off balance. "People who are victims are diminished. . . . You feel, emotionally, you must have done something wrong, or that something is wrong with you," noted Ervin Staub, a University of Massachusetts psychology professor who has worked extensively in postgenocidal Rwanda. Because we tend to "see the world as a just place," he added, "people who suffer [often feel they] must somehow deserve it." They see their misfortune as "God's punishment." Having the wrongdoer accept responsibility is a step in the process of putting things in perspective. And apology takes it a step beyond. Forgiveness is yet another possible step. "Under the right conditions, people can move to a position of acceptance of each other, including acceptance of what the other has done," said Staub, author of *The Roots of Evil*.

Theologians and philosophers have long recognized the power behind the ritual of apology and forgiveness. The leap made by the TRC was to believe that what applied to individuals could apply to nations and groups within nations as well, that the bringing together of the wrongdoer and aggrieved could, under the proper circumstances, lead to healing that went far beyond the particular people reconciling.

In the past few years, we have seen an outbreak of apologies. Polish President Aleksander Kwasniewski and a group of Polish bishops apologized for a massacre of Jews in 1941. The New Zealand prime minister apologized for the 1918 introduction of Spanish influenza into Western Samoa. The Canadian government apologized for its abuse of its indigenous population. President Bill Clinton apologized for "The Tuskegee Study of Untreated Syphilis in the Negro Male." And the list goes on, as does the list of those demanding apologies—for Japanese sexual slavery during World War II, for American slavery, for European colonialism.

Do such apologies matter? Mary Robinson, former president of Ireland, believes that they do. When we spoke in 2001, during her tenure as United Nations High Commissioner for Human Rights, Robinson recalled the letter British Prime Minister Tony Blair had sent in 1997 expressing sorrow for those who had died in the Irish potato famine of the 1840s. "That one million people should have died in what was then part of the richest and most powerful nation in the world is something that still causes pain as we reflect on it today. Those who governed in London at the time failed their people through standing by while a crop failure turned into a massive human tragedy," he wrote.

Blair's action was "an event talked about in clubs and pubs," said Robinson. "It made a difference." How could an apology a century and a half after the fact conceivably matter? If psychologist Robert Enright is right, it's because the "wounds of the earlier generation" continue to fester in the current generation.

Kirkland Vaughans, a friend and clinical psychologist, confided during a conversation that he had become fascinated with the cross-generational transmission of attitudes. He had noticed that his European immigrant clients and his African American clients had totally different takes on the child welfare system and laws. Some of the Europeans resented those policies because they thought they denied them the right to properly discipline—or beat—their children. Many African Americans resented them because they thought those laws could be used to take their children away. Why the difference? He wasn't sure but wondered whether it didn't have something to do with the black American experience under slavery when children could be taken at the whim of an owner and parents had no rights.

Why are aboriginal people around the world demanding apologies and satisfaction for actions that go back decades and, in some cases, centuries? Why are some black Americans obsessed with the idea of reparations for slavery? Why do people insist that memories of the Holocaust be kept alive? The answer, of course, is that the past matters. It shapes the present no less than a mother shapes a child.

To what extent can we correct the wrongs of the past? How, in both a personal and political sense, can we confront and conquer the pain of past wounds? What does it mean to reconcile—or even to peacefully coexist—as individuals, as groups, as nations? Can a model of reconciliation appropriate for friends, lovers, or members of a family—rooted in the catharsis of confession, coupled ideally with acknowledgment, maybe apology, and if God smiles, forgiveness—work when there are no close ties?

Writing in the October 12, 2001, issue of the *National Catholic*

Reporter, journalist William Bole observed that today's ethnic and religious conflicts were "highly resistant to the standard remedies of realism" and suggested that perhaps "a radical new factor, such as forgiveness" was needed: "For us in the United States, forgiving those responsible for the slaughter of September 11 is nearly unthinkable. But what of the wider populations from which these terrorists came with their desperate hatred of the United States? Could we afford not to embark on a journey of forgiveness and reconciliation with these communities?"

Forgiveness is not always possible, nor is reconciliation. They are concepts grounded largely in religion that, depending on the situation, may require a level of compassion or a brand of spirituality that many of us don't have; or they may require an effort many of us are not prepared to make. As a friend and a daughter of Holocaust survivors suggested, sometimes it may make sense to hold on to outrage. Some would argue that certain wrongs can only be repaid with revenge.

Are some things so horrible—the September 11 tragedy, for instance, the abuse of children, perhaps—that they provide no context in which to even consider reconciliation? And where reconciliation is possible, must it be preceded by atonement? And, if so, how does one atone for past actions? How does a country, how do a people, atone for past deeds? Do demands for reparations and the trend toward truth commissions represent meaningful ways of dealing with the past? Is the need to remember necessarily at odds with the need to move on? Does social justice sometimes demand the settling of scores? Does this new movement to recover memories, to recover history, represent an important change for better in the world? I will consider those issues in due course, along with several related others. But let us stay for a while on forgiveness, which has lately been the source of a lot of new work and a lot of new hope and which, as Nethercut discovered, is a richly paradoxical phenomenon: an act impelled by selflessness whose primary beneficiary is likely to be oneself.

1.

DECIDING TO FORGIVE

To forgive the truly horrible is to kiss the robe of God, to emulate no less a figure than the dying Jesus Christ. *Father, forgive them; for they know not what they do.* Those words leapt into Colleen Kelly's mind when she realized her brother was gone forever, buried in the smoldering graveyard that had once been the World Trade Center. The architectural pride of Wall Street, an icon of America's power and beauty, was now a symbol of incomprehensible horror, an unlikely resting place for Bill.

Bill was in financial services, a salesman for Bloomberg L.P. He did not normally work at the World Trade Center. So the family initially had no idea he was there. But once the planes plowed into the towers, New Yorkers everywhere picked up phones, mostly to reassure one another life would go on.

Colleen learned that Bill had been attending a conference at Windows on the World, the restaurant on the 107th floor of the World Trade Center. And that September day it fell on her, a nurse and mother of three living in the Bronx, to make the trek into Manhattan. Sustained by the hope, the dream, that Bill had somehow made it out, she wandered from hospital to hospital, inquiring about her brother. Eventually she grew cognizant of an ominous fact: though doctors and nurses abounded, there was no one for them to treat—no one, at any rate, from the World Trade Center. "That's when I knew Bill was dead." And that's when the words of Jesus Christ flashed through her mind. *Father, forgive them; for they know not what they do.*

She realized the words made absolutely no sense, not in the present context. The terrorists had clearly known, with horrifying precision, exactly what it was that they were doing. Her response, she later concluded, stemmed not from an urge to forgive but from an almost instinctive resolve not to hate. The leap to Jesus' words on the cross was her mind's way of reaffirming values that she had clung to all her life, values that embraced peace over war. In the face of the most wrenching provocation imaginable, she rejected vengeance. "These terrorists had taken my brother," she told me over lunch many months later, "and I wasn't going to let them take anything else."

Colleen was among the founders of September Eleventh Families for Peaceful Tomorrows. The families sought to honor their lost loved ones by condemning vengeance and violence— even if that meant visiting Iraq as America prepared to make war on Saddam Hussein, or meeting with the mother of Zacarias Moussaoui (the so-called twentieth hijacker) in an effort at dialogue and reconciliation.

It is not my purpose here to consider the political effectiveness or appropriateness of such efforts. I am more interested in Kelly's initial impulse, in the notion that forgiveness, albeit as a proxy for a larger set of values, could even be considered in the context of acts so vile as those perpetrated by the September 11 terrorists.

Are some things so awful they cannot be forgiven? Or does wisdom lie closer to Kelly's instinctive response? Are some acts so horrifying, so incomprehensible, so beyond the scope of normal humanity, that they must be forgiven—or at least consigned to that section of the heart most open to mercy and compassion, most inclined to let go of the urge to revenge?

A developing school of psychology argues that forgiveness is a gift not only to the person forgiven but to those who grant the gift, those strong enough to forgive. Robert Enright, a leader in that school, sees forgiveness as a route to personal freedom, a way of rejecting the self-imposed, self-reinforcing label of victim and escaping an ultimately soul-destroying maze of anger and resentment. Indeed, practicing forgiveness may even lower your blood pressure, while relieving other ailments—physical and mental—traceable to the stress of chronic anger.

It is not just a handful of psychologists, but also holy men and philosophers, who trumpet the benefits of a forgiving soul, who see forgiveness as much of the answer to what is wrong with mankind. Like all true believers, they overreach; many would turn the whole world into the church of forgiveness. And they tend to seek converts where they cannot (and perhaps should not) be found. But I believe they are onto something important—at least for those capable of or willing to take on the challenge of living the attitude these particular believers promote.

In *Forgiveness Is a Choice* Enright tries to explain what forgiveness is and what it is not. It is not giving up the ability to hold people accountable or letting wrongdoers off the hook. It does not mean forgetting the wrong that they did, or becoming complicit in continued abuse. It does not mean turning your head as a pedophile abuses children or a violent husband batters his wife. Instead—and he borrows the definition from philosopher Joanna North—forgiveness means responding to unjust hurt with compassion, with benevolence, perhaps even with love. While it does not deny the right to resentment, it does not wallow in bitterness; nor does it necessarily demand that the perpetrator respond with gratitude or grace. Or as Enright and Richard Fitzgibbons spell it out in *Helping Clients Forgive*, "People, upon rationally determining that they have been unfairly treated, forgive when they willfully abandon resentment and related responses (to which they have a right), and endeavor to respond to the wrongdoer based on the moral principle of beneficence, which may include compassion, unconditional worth, generosity, and moral love (to which the wrongdoer, by nature of the harmful acts, has no right)." Michael McCullough, another psychologist and forgiveness researcher, defines the concept considerably less grandly—as ending estrangement and letting go of resentments and of the urge to revenge.

Granting the kind of forgiveness Enright endorses seems a tall order for a mere mortal—even one who hopes it will lower her blood pressure and otherwise make her a better, more healthy human specimen. Yet I have repeatedly found myself amazed at the capacity of and willingness of otherwise ordinary human beings to return injury with compassion.

Consider Azim Khamisa, an elegant, international investment financial consultant who is of Persian and Indian lineage. Khamisa was born in Kenya, educated in England, and immigrated to the United States in 1974. He was living in La Jolla, California, in January 1995 when tragedy shattered his theretofore peaceful existence.

After returning from a business trip to Mexico City, Khamisa had gone directly to a party. Having just endured a painful breakup with his then-girlfriend, Khamisa was soaking in the warmth and goodwill from a group of people particularly close to him. Khamisa and his friends left the party together and went to his home. Once they departed, an exhausted Khamisa collapsed in bed; he apparently slept through the knocks on the door later that night. The next morning, Sunday, his maid brought him a business card from a policeman—a homicide detective—that had been left in his door.

Khamisa called. It was then that he received the heart-stopping news that Tariq, his son, was dead. At first, Khamisa refused to believe it. The news was so shocking, so unexpected that he simply couldn't accept it. He hung up, dialed Tariq's number, and waited with every expectation that his son would come on the line. Instead, Tariq's fiancée answered, sobbing.

At that moment, the truth sank in. It was as if a nuclear bomb had exploded inside, tearing him into a million pieces, recalled Khamisa. "Life drained out of me." His soul left his body, ascending to another plane. "I felt the long arms of my Maker."

In time, Khamisa's soul returned, and he had no choice but to face facts. Tariq, then twenty and a student at San Diego State University, had been at his pizza delivery job that Saturday night when a woman ordered a pizza. Her call aroused no particular suspicions, nor did the delivery address—a building in a lower-middle-class community not far from the university. When Tariq arrived, however, he found that the given apartment number did not exist.

Four gang members lay in wait. They pounced as Tariq headed back to the car. He made it inside, but the eighteen-year-old gang leader was not about to let him go. "Bust him," he ordered a fourteen-year-old soldier. The bullet passed through the window, through Tariq's shoulder, underneath one arm and came out under the other. The youths fled. A priest in a nearby building heard the shot and rushed out of the shower and into the street. He tried CPR, but Tariq, his aorta ruptured, was already dead.

One of Khamisa's close friends had also lost a son to murder. In an effort to comfort the grief-stricken Khamisa, the friend expressed the hope that Tariq's killers would "fry in hell." He also talked about his own lost son, and about how, if he could only get his hands on the murderer, he would execute not just the killer but "his whole clan." To Khamisa, who harbored no lust for revenge, the confession brought no relief.

He buried his son that Thursday. "My rage came on Friday," Khamisa recalled. "I was angry, but not at Tony [the shooter]," he told me. His anger singled out no particular individual; it was something more generalized, aimed at whatever it was in American society that had produced a fourteen-year-old kid who had killed a stranger on command. "My rage was mostly directed at society and my country." For the eighth-grade murderer, he felt compassion.

Khamisa's religious beliefs played a role in his reaction. A Shiite Muslim, Khamisa belongs to the Ismaili sect and extols Sufism—an "inner, mystical, or psycho-spiritual dimension of Islam," in the words of Alan Godlas, a scholar at the University of Georgia. Khamisa's faith is "more eastern, more Buddhist than fundamentalist." It is about a quest for "the hidden meaning in the faith," Khamisa explained.

That faith, as Khamisa practices it, embraces peace, forgiveness, love; and it doesn't allow much time for mourning or for self-pity. "We mourn the first forty days. After forty days, excessive mourning will impede the soul's journey," Khamisa's Ismaili spiritual adviser reminded him. The adviser also told him that his response to the death of his son would determine the quality of the rest of his life.

Those words spawned a great deal of solitary soul-searching, some of it spent on Mammoth Mountain, immersed in nature's tranquility. Khamisa struggled with a dilemma. "I wanted to do something for my son; but how do you do something for somebody who's not here?"

"This was a meaningless tragedy, very random. Tony and Tariq had never met. But for me to continue the rest of my life"— Khamisa paused as he gathered his thoughts—"how do you do this without taking it and making some meaning out of it?" He continued, "I had lost my will to live."

The answer came that April; he would form a foundation in his son's memory. The Tariq Khamisa Foundation tries to save people like the fourteen-year-old Tony Hicks, an alienated kid who committed murder for lack of something better to do. It holds forums in schools to teach kids the consequences of violence. The hope is that young people will learn how "to make the kind of choices that Tony did not make," said Khamisa. "If he had gone through this program, he would have made different choices," Khamisa added. As it was, Hicks ended up pleading guilty to first-degree murder and was given a sentence of twenty-five years to life. He was the first juvenile to be sentenced as an adult under a new law aimed at young offenders.

The foundation "may not bring my child back; but we're going to stop other children from dying," vowed Khamisa.

When we spoke in early 2003, Khamisa noted that the foundation had grown to the point where it had a six-person staff, including his daughter, who was twenty-two when Tariq was killed. Since launching the foundation, Khamisa has received grateful letters from thousands of young people. "They help to mitigate the loss," he said. Khamisa had also noticed some changes in himself: "I'm a better person as a result of this tragedy . . . more compassionate, less self-indulgent."

The killer, Tony Hicks, had also undergone a transformation. Initially Hicks, as Khamisa tells it, was unrepentant. "He thought the pizza delivery man was stupid." But in the months leading up to his sentencing, Hicks's feelings changed. He ultimately begged for Khamisa's forgiveness.

Meanwhile, Khamisa developed a relationship with Hicks's grandfather and guardian, Ples Felix, who was nearly as traumatized by his grandson's choices as was Khamisa by the death of his son. The two men forged an alliance and they now appear onstage together, promoting nonviolence in Tariq's name. Khamisa dreams of the day when he, the grandfather, and Hicks, who may be paroled in 2017, can appear together to tell the story of the events that have forever changed and connected their lives.

"Azim's journey is a testament to the power of forgiveness. Through that power, we both rose up from the devastation that struck us down," wrote Ples Felix in the afterword to *From Murder to Forgiveness,* the book Khamisa published about his son's murder and its consequences. As for Tariq, the foundation was contributing to his spiritual life. It was building up "millions and millions of dollars of spiritual currency" in his name, said Khamisa. "Maybe Tariq will complete the rest of his journey in a Learjet."

Khamisa is an exceptional man. And yet he is not all that different from Richard Nethercut, or from Marietta Jaeger, who managed to reach out, in a spirit of conciliation and forgiveness, to the man who had kidnapped her daughter.

That kidnapping took place during the summer of 1972. Jaeger was in Montana on a camping vacation with her family when her seven-year-old daughter, the youngest child of five, was taken from the tent. When family members finally awakened and realized she was missing, they knew that she had not wandered off. Susie was much too well schooled to do such a thing. And when they saw that the tent had been cut, they had no choice but to assume that she had been abducted.

The response from the authorities, and even from ordinary people, was amazing and overwhelming. Soldiers with tracking dogs, private pilots with their own planes, and countless others— most just ordinary people willing to search on foot—showed up and offered their help. Businesses also contributed by releasing employees for the search. But despite all the assistance and good wishes, nothing turned up.

A week or so after Susie disappeared, the killer called the FBI. To confirm his identity, he mentioned a detail—Susie's deformed fingernail—that had not been publicly disclosed. He demanded $50,000 to be left in a bus depot in a locker; but he neglected to say exactly where or how the money should be delivered. The instructions were so maddeningly vague that Jaeger held a press conference to ask the kidnapper to please get in touch again.

It was around that time, said Jaeger, that she realized how much she had repressed her anger. She had simply not allowed it to surface. Suddenly, the damned-up rage crashed through. "Until that point," she recalled, "it had not occurred to me to be angry."

That all changed. "I allowed myself to get in touch with my anger, and I realized I had every right to feel the way I did. . . . I was just ravaged with hatred and a desire for revenge."

One night as she and her husband prepared for bed, Jaeger turned to him, consumed with anger, and said, "If the kidnapper were to bring Susie back alive and well, I could kill him." "And I knew I could," she said years later, "with my bare hands and a smile on my face." She was shaken by her own reaction. A "wrestling match with God and my conscience" ensued.

Jaeger was raised a Catholic. Hatred was unholy. To give into rage, decided Jaeger, would be to diminish herself and her relationship with God. So she "made a decision to make a commitment to forgiveness, to work toward forgiveness."

When the police and FBI came up empty, Jaeger returned to her home in Michigan. A few months later, the kidnapper called a second time, reaching Jaeger's sixteen-year-old son. The kidnapper repeated the demand for ransom but again hung up without giving coherent instructions.

A period of intense frustration followed. Clues emerged that led nowhere. Hopes were raised only to come crashing to earth. Jaeger renewed her faith. She continued to reject hatred and revenge. However she felt about the kidnapper, "in God's eyes, he was just as precious as my little girl," she told herself. Also, as a Christian, she was called on to pray for her enemies. So she forced herself to say little prayers on the kidnapper's behalf. If he is fishing, prayed Jaeger, let him have good weather, let him catch plenty of fish. All the while, she held on to the hope that her daughter was alive, and that the kidnapper would get in touch and that the nightmare would end. As the one-year anniversary of the kidnapping approached, a reporter from Montana called. She would "do anything," Jaeger told the reporter, for the chance to talk to the kidnapper. The reporter published her statement.

In June 1974, a year to the date of the abduction, the kidnapper called a third time. He started out by taunting Jaeger, but she ignored his taunts. "My primary concern was to reach the man. Find out who he was, why he had done this. How to get her back. . . . I felt like I was standing outside, watching myself. . . . I just desperately wanted to make a human contact with him."

"What can I do to help you?" she asked at one point. The kidnapper did not answer directly. Instead, he said something along the lines of "I wish this burden could be lifted from me." Jaeger realized that her words had touched him; his mood was very different from what it had been when the conversation began. They ended up talking for nearly an hour, during which the man made increasingly self-incriminating statements.

The clues he dropped led her to realize that he was one of the suspects who had been picked up originally, a twenty-six-year-old with a troubled emotional past. After he had passed a lie detector test, the authorities had let him go for lack of evidence. They had kept him under surveillance, but he had managed to slip out of Montana and drive to Salt Lake City, from where he had called Jaeger, confident the call could never be traced back to him. Eventually she started to call him by his name, which so rattled him that he vowed, "You'll never see your little girl alive again," and slammed down the phone.

He reappeared in his hometown a short while later, insisting he had never left. But the conversation, which she had taped, was evidence enough for the cops to get search warrants. They combed through an abandoned ranch not far from where he lived. There they found the remains of an eighteen-year-old female, along with the backbone of a small girl. Apparently Susie had been dead all along, killed perhaps a week after being kidnapped.

The kidnapper was arrested but initially denied involvement. Eventually—after the prosecutor, prodded by Jaeger, took the death penalty off the table—he confessed to Susie's murder and three others. Days later, he committed suicide by hanging himself.

Jaeger and her family quietly buried "what little was left of

Susie." Later, she sought out the mother of the murderer. "Maybe it would be helpful to her to know I had forgiven him," she figured. "Together we were able to grieve for the loss of our children." To this day, the woman remains a friend.

In 1998, Jaeger returned to Montana, to commemorate the twenty-fifth anniversary of her daughter's death. Her first husband, Susie's father, had died. And during that visit she met a cattle rancher. They married. She moved permanently to Montana and now lives outside the town where Susie disappeared.

Patricia Stonestreet, an elegant, gray-haired interior designer from Houston, Texas, had a strikingly similar experience. In June 1986, as she was getting ready to leave her office, she got a call telling her that her twenty-eight-year-old daughter, Lisa, was dead. At that moment a part of the mother died as well: "I felt like I was in a pit . . . screaming."

A twenty-five-year-old truck driver—who as it turned out had raped numerous other women—had broken into Lisa's apartment, raped her, stabbed her in the eyes, strangled her with pantyhose, and ultimately drowned her in the bathtub. Authorities found the slender, dark-haired beauty slumped over the bathtub, her head submerged in water. The assailant, Kenneth Bernard Harris, blamed his crack cocaine addiction for his acts.

The night of Lisa's funeral, recalled her mother, "My husband said, out of the clear blue, we have to forgive that man. . . . We felt it would benefit us greatly if we followed the Scriptures and did what the Bible commanded us to do."

Harris, who was originally scheduled to die in 1995, got a stay of execution. Lee, Patricia Stonestreet's husband, died the following year—of a "broken heart," she believes. Nonetheless, the family stayed firm in its resolve to forgive.

"We wanted to let him know we had forgiven him. It wasn't for revenge; it wasn't for closure. . . . There is no closure for a victim."

The rules of the penitentiary prohibited them from making

direct contact with the murderer. So when he had a new execution date set—June 1997—Stonestreet and her three remaining
children decided to attend. Before Harris died they would let him
know he was forgiven.

They wrote the words "We forgive you" on a three-by-five
card, which they planned to show him. But they were told no such
display would be allowed. A chaplain, however, took Harris the
message; and when the curtain opened, he asked to make a statement.

"I am sorry for all of the pain I have caused both families—my
family and yours," he said.

Even though forgiveness allowed the Stonestreet family to let
go of the anger, it did not take away the pain. The healing, said
Stonestreet, took years. And it was facilitated by her decision to
volunteer for Bridges to Life, a faith-based program in Texas that
sends crime victims into prisons. Over a twelve-week period, victims share their stories with the aim of helping the inmates realize
the deep damage they have done. Since starting her work with
Bridges in 1998, Stonestreet said, she had participated in the program, as of June 2003, some twenty-three times: "We heal a little
bit when we tell our stories."

Marietta Jaeger (now Marietta Jaeger Lane), Azim Khamisa,
and Patricia Stonestreet found solace in their respective faiths.
Indeed, to some substantial extent, their reactions were dictated
by their faiths. But their behavior was not dictated by faith alone.
Religious obligations can be interpreted in any number of ways;
and neither most Shiites nor most Christians respond to murder
by expressing compassion for the murderer. *Vengeance is mine . . .
saith the Lord.* And when it comes to the particularly horrible,
many of us are just as content to let Him do His own forgiving as
well. The choices made by Khamisa and Jaeger Lane and
Stonestreet, I suspect, have at least as much to do with the kinds
of human beings they are as with the brands of faith they happen
to practice.

For Robert Enright and his forgiveness-minded colleagues, religion is not exactly beside the point, but it is subsumed under a much broader set of human dynamics. "Forgiveness . . . transcends the narrowly religious or denominational" but is "of profound spiritual and moral relevance to all of us, regardless of whether we hold specifically religious beliefs," wrote philosopher Joanna North in an essay in *Exploring Forgiveness,* a book she coedited with Enright.

Obeying religious principles is only one of countless possible human motivations for walking down the path of forgiveness. There are those who want to save or resurrect a relationship with a parent, a lover, or a spouse. And the price of resurrection is often forgiveness—a forgiveness that, in some sense, may be harder to grant than forgiveness to a stranger. For a stranger, even a stranger who murders your daughter, had no relationship with you to violate. He committed a terrible act; but there was no betrayal of trust, since he had been granted no trust to violate.

In *Exploring Forgiveness*, Joanna North takes on the question of why a woman might forgive someone who attacked and robbed her. Certainly the woman would be justified in feeling contempt for her attacker. But what if years later she is still feeling the effects of that attack, if she is "anxious, nervous, depressed, suspicious, and mistrustful," if the "attack has corrupted and all but destroyed her life . . . because she cannot let go of the pain, cannot forgive the man who attacked her." Through forgiveness, argues North, "the pain and hurt caused by the original wrong are released, or at least they are not allowed to mar the whole of one's being for all time."

For close relations—a mother, a lover, a spouse—things are considerably different. One is not seeking merely to be released from pain, but also to understand, deepen, and perhaps redefine a relationship. And it is that very relationship that makes the offense worse—that, in some cases, even makes the offense possible. *You cannot be abandoned by a stranger whom you never expected to know.* And though rape under any circumstances is horrible, rape by a father is infinitely worse. And that relationship is also what complicates the question of forgiveness.

The process of, the motivation for, and the expectations of forgiveness are different when dealing with a stranger who emerged from the night. Consider two stories, one told to me by a psychologist and therapist, the other by a woman struggling, in the most personal way, with the weight of betrayal and the possibility of reconciliation.

It was not so long ago that Sharon, as we will call her, used to cut herself—small cuts with a razor where they would not be seen, on her upper arms, on her inner thighs, places covered by clothing. Painful though the cuts were, they were nothing compared to the pain inside from which the self-mutilation provided a release. "When she cut herself, it was as if the pain left her," said her therapist.

Pretty, athletic, with thick, dark hair, Sharon was sixteen when she came into therapy. On the surface, things could not have been better. She was an A student in advance-placement classes at her exclusive prep school, a standout in three sports, the kind of child that causes parents to puff up with pride. All that was lost on her mother—an alcoholic divorcee, who had been rejecting Sharon virtually since the moment of her birth.

The most memorable brush-off occurred when Sharon was eleven. Her mother, in the throes of an alcoholic rage, chased her out of her house and tossed Sharon's clothes out behind her. Frightened and confused, Sharon waited on the front lawn until her father, called by a neighbor, appeared and rescued her.

Her dad, already estranged from the mother at the time of the incident, won Sharon in the divorce. The two younger girls stayed with their mom. "I was never what my mother wanted," confided Sharon. "I'm not blond and skinny with blue eyes; I'm a dark-haired Jew who's a lesbian."

Her two sisters, who were indeed blond and blue-eyed, took after their mother, while Sharon was cast in the image of her father.

And though her father loved her unconditionally, her mother's rejection ate away at her. "The anger was so overwhelming, it debilitated her," observed her therapist. A friend, who had noticed the cutting, had prodded her into therapy. And not a moment too soon, as the therapist saw it.

"Cutting is a real tricky thing. And kids who do it are clever at knowing where to do it. But she was getting awful close to where she should not have been cutting." It did not take the therapist long to ascertain that the root problem was Sharon's mother, who thought nothing of disrupting her daughters' lives for her own purposes, even to the point of bringing false charges of child sexual abuse against the children's father.

During her first year in therapy, Sharon improved dramatically. Her depression lifted—in part due to antidepressant drugs—and she stopped cutting herself. She also began to feel better about herself, a process helped immeasurably by the incredible support her classmates gave her when she came out as a lesbian. Most dramatically, her attitude toward her mother changed. She went from rage and resentment to a state of partial understanding,

Her mother's behavior, Sharon decided, was really not totally her mother's fault. The woman was trapped by forces, including her drinking, beyond her control. So Sharon forgave her mother. And the change was astounding. She went from being an angry, self-destructive teenager to someone whose face reflected an inner sense of peace. "The burden of anger, of not forgiving, is more powerful sometimes than the trauma that causes the damage. Carrying around hurt and anger absorbs an enormous amount of energy," observed the therapist. So though she supported the decision to forgive, she was wary of Sharon's impulse to reestablish a relationship with her mother. The therapist had seen too many cases of abused children all too eager to embrace an abusive parent just so they could return to what they considered a state of normalcy.

Forgiveness, of course, does not necessitate acceptance of the unacceptable. It does not mean excusing abuse. In many cases, it makes sense only if forgiveness is part of a "larger package of understanding," noted Paula Panzer, a trauma expert and psychiatrist with the Jewish Board of Family and Children's Services in New York. "If I don't also know that my inability to concentrate at work, or my subsequent dating problems, or my stomachache, or my drinking problem is related to trauma, forgiving is not going to solve those other problems," Panzer pointed out.

Indeed, for some who have decided to forgive, that decision itself can create conflict—especially if the object of one's intended forgiveness is considered unworthy.

Consider Amy's dilemma. Like Sharon, Amy, as I will call her, was seeking a new relationship with her mother; and she, likewise, was dealing with issues of abuse. A petite redhead whose irrepressibly friendly manner gives no sign of a childhood spent in hell, Amy was raised in a Mormon household that, at least superficially, was deeply devout. Her mother was the head of the women's auxiliary and extremely active in the church.

Amy is not precisely sure when the abuse began. She was either six or seven. Her father, nearly three hundred pounds, was a frightening, chronically angry man. Initially, he fondled her; but he eventually tried to have intercourse. He stopped only because of the bleeding and the noise. "I screamed so loud, he decided not to hurt me."

He did not, however, stop the abuse. He continued fondling her and subsequently moved on to oral sex. He kept it up until she was fourteen and finally summoned the nerve to fight. When he would touch her, she would kick, scratch, do whatever she could to make him leave her alone. Eventually he gave up and Amy kept his secret. She felt she had no choice. If their "affair," as he termed it, became public, he warned, the family would disintegrate. Having seen the effects of divorce on her aunt's family, she knew it was nothing she wanted to cause. So she kept quiet: "I felt a responsibility to keep the family together."

Amy believes the abuse tainted her entire childhood. A pale red-head with a translucent complexion, she stood out at her mixed-raced school. Many kids, especially the Latinos, taunted her. But her father had sapped so much of her spirit that she could never fight back.

It wasn't until she got married—at the age of sixteen—to another domineering, older man—that she began to feel safe. She quickly started a family of her own. At the time, her sister, who was five years younger than Amy, was still living with her parents in the trailer across the street. Amy had never imagined that her father would dare abuse another child; but one day when she walked into the trailer, she saw her sister, then thirteen, emerge from their father's room. "I just thought, 'No way. She's not going to go through that,' " said Amy, who by then had two children of her own.

Struggling to stay calm, Amy pulled her younger sister aside and told her how their father had violated her. "Is he abusing you?" she asked as tears flooded her sister's eyes.

Her anguished expression gave the answer. The abuse had gone on for as long as she could remember, the sister confided. "I was totally shattered," recalled Amy. "Something welled up in me I had never experienced before." She marched into her father's room and yelled, *"It's over.* You will never do it again to my sister. I don't care what you do to me. You can kill me, but I'm turning you in."

Amy was terrified; she had seen her father pummel her brothers and put his fist through a door. He was capable of smacking her, perhaps capable of killing her. And she feared the worse. But instead of striking out, he collapsed within, and he cried, begging her forgiveness. "I don't blame you. Go ahead. I need help," he said.

She turned in her father to the bishop of her church. The church elders ordered the father into counseling and advised Amy to keep her mouth shut. It was important, they told her, to "allow your father to repent without being judged by our community."

Now she realizes the church erred in not sending the whole family into counseling. When she did get counseling on her own, the therapist's advice contradicted that of the elders'. "He encouraged me to get it out in the open."

She believes the abuse and subsequent trauma undermined— and ultimately ruined—her first marriage. During the marriage, she struggled with "insecurities, horrible jealousy issues . . . I was hypersensitive . . . constantly watching for any kind of reason to suspect." And when her husband touched her in the night she would respond as she had to her father as a child—hitting, kicking, scratching, instinctively defending herself. After the battle with her father over her sister, things got worse at her own home. "My husband wasn't aware of the abuse. And when he found out, it changed the way he looked at me. . . . He felt betrayed that I hadn't been honest with him prior to the marriage."

Nonetheless, said Amy, "I forgave my father early on." His upbringing had been horrible, she reasoned. He was an orphan, and his guardians had beat him with a horsewhip. He had been made to drive cattle in the snow with holes in his shoes and he had been forced to work in the middle of the night, feeding the mink on which the family relied for a livelihood. "If I had been raised like that, I might have done what he had done," she said.

Amy's empathy notwithstanding, her dad did not make forgiveness easy. "Once I had forgiven him, he wouldn't let it go. . . . He would keep asking my forgiveness. . . . I wanted to move on. I didn't want to keep experiencing it. I wanted to create something new with my father, and I never did, which I regret."

Although forgiving her father was relatively easy, forgiving her mother was not. How, she wondered, had her mother allowed the situation to continue? Why had Mom signed up for night classes, knowing her departure would leave Amy alone with her dad? How could her mother deny culpability when, on one occasion, she walked in as dad performed oral sex? "She cried all night," Amy recalled. "I know because I was on the other side of that door. You can't tell me she didn't see it."

Amy tried to be proactively positive. She consumed personal improvement books for tips on dealing with her pain and she found work in the personal empowerment field, leading seminars to help men and women take control of their lives. She refused to feel sorry for herself. "I will *never* again be a victim," she said.

Still, nearly a quarter of a century after the abuse, she still seethed at the thought of her mother's betrayal. Some years ago she tried to talk it out with her mother. But her mom continued to plead ignorance, refusing to accept any responsibility. "To this day, she has not come to me with remorse," said Amy.

She found a life coach who was "able to show me what a frightened person my mother must have been to risk her daughter's physical, emotional, and mental well-being, for the sake of appearances." As a result, said Amy, "I've forgiven her. I don't understand it; but I don't feel the need so much now." Yet the forgiveness is far from complete. "I need to move beyond accepting it . . . to compassion for my mother," she said. "When I sit and think about it, I can go there. And then when I *experience* my mom . . ." Her voice trailed off. Through much of here life, she added, she had felt that her mom was jealous of her. "My mother says she loves me, but it's like it's out of duty. . . . Even her hugs feel mechanical. They didn't feel genuine and they still don't."

Given Amy's plainly conflicted feelings, why did she feel such an obligation to forgive? "In the end," she replied, "I don't think there's any true healing, unless it all heals."

Can she ever get to that point of forgiveness? Should she? The answer to the first is almost certainly yes, though it is easy to see why the journey has been so difficult. She had no basis for understanding her mother, nor any reason to feel particularly charitable toward her. And when I interviewed her in early 2003, she had yet to receive anything remotely resembling an apology. "Without an acknowledgment of what the perpetrator did and an expression of regret, to forgive is complicated," observed Ervin Staub, the University of Massachusetts psychologist.

Still, even in the absence of contrition, forgiveness is possible. Indeed, Enright's prescription for forgiveness does not assume the perpetrator meets the victim halfway, or even that she cares whether she is forgiven or not. He believes forgiveness is worth the effort, quite apart from anything the guilty or offending party might do. And that effort, as laid out in four stages and numerous steps within those stages, is considerable.

Those stages, conceptually, are straightforward enough. First comes the acknowledgment of anger; for anger—and its effects on a person's mental and emotional well-being—must be acknowledged before it can be effectively assuaged. In acknowledging the hurt or betrayal, in stripping away the defenses that keep pain at bay, you must be prepared for the resurfacing, the reliving, of trauma as scars that never properly healed are exposed anew.

Second comes the decision to forgive. Implicit in that decision is a commitment to forgo even small attempts at revenge. Enright suggests that you might want to come up with your own definition of forgiveness, one that fits the particular circumstances of your case. At any rate, in the second stage, you are opening yourself up to the possibility of answering abuse with compassion.

The third stage begins the process of implementing the decision to forgive, which most likely means engaging the person who caused your distress. It is also the phase in which you accept the pain but then begin to move on, perhaps with the help of God. You may try to put yourself in the other person's shoes. You may even offer a gift, a small token, such as a greeting card, symbolizing the rejection of rancor.

Fourth, and finally, comes forgiveness itself, accompanied by the release, as Enright puts it, from the "emotional prison." In emerging from that prison you might find a new focus in life. You might find a way, as Khamisa put it, of "making some meaning" out of adversity. And you may also find it possible to say "I forgive you" and to mean it, as Richard Nethercut did, when he was able to purge his heart of anything other than goodwill toward the man who had murdered his daughter.

The obvious question is "Why bother?" Even if forgiving does make you feel better, the road is so arduous, the process potentially so difficult. There must be easier ways to release oneself from emotional turmoil than to embrace the one who harmed you. And what of those like Amy, who have already been deeply traumatized by wrongdoing or betrayal? Dare we risk making them feel even worse by insisting they forgive the transgressor?

"Society often tells us that revenge is unhealthy and that our only way for peace is through forgiveness. However, we victims feel this is another of society's guilt trips. . . . Forgive if you must, but do not allow these insensitive people to shame it from you." That defiant declaration is on the website of an online victims support group called DOVE (Dignity of Victims Everywhere).

Richard Cress is the man behind the website. His thirteen-year-old son was murdered in 1983 and left in a ditch. The killers were never found. Cress got little solace from a victims' group he joined in the Seattle area, so he subsequently formed his own support group, which evolved into the online service it is now. Cress does not much believe in forgiveness and reconciliation, not when it involves people like those who took the life of his son: "Restorative justice is fine when it deals with nonviolent crime," he said, but when dealing with people who have committed horrible acts of violence, forgiveness makes no sense. A person who murders is likely to do it again, he believes; and therefore revenge—execution—is the most reasonable response. If the persons who killed his son were caught: "I would give [the lethal injection] to them myself. . . . I would like nothing better."

Some truth commissions—and in particular the one in South Africa—have been criticized for making a fetish of forgiveness, for orchestrating scenes where forgiveness is so expected that it is essentially coerced, and is therefore granted, whatever the victim's true feelings or needs may be. The magic of animosity evaporating, the symbolism of former enemies embracing, trumps any qualms about whether the reconciliation is real.

In *A Human Being Died That Night,* Pumla Gobodo-Madikizela, a psychologist who served on South Africa's TRC, recounts the story of Winnie Mandela's appearance at a TRC hearing. The TRC was investigating Mandela's role in the murder and torture of young black men in Soweto. The commission was particularly interested in how it was that a youth named Stompie Seipei came to be killed. This is Pumla Gobodo-Madikizela's account:

> *At the end of the public hearing, during which Madikizela-Mandela essentially denied any knowledge of what had been happening in her own backyard, and offered no meaningful apology, she approached Stompie Seipei's mother while the TV cameras rolled. With a triumphant smile and open arms, she embraced her. I watched the moment of contact between the two women: the mother's humble smile and return of the gesture, and Madikizela-Mandela's triumphant smile, enacting her imposing power through her embrace. Two smiles: one a symbol of power, and the other a symbol of impotence.*
>
> *Stompie Seipei's bereaved mother had sat for nine days at the public hearing of the TRC looking silence in the face as Madikizela-Mandela revealed nothing, ending where she had started, with more silence. Yet she opened her arms to receive the embrace of this woman who was prepared to offer nothing beyond flat denial. It was an embrace that stripped the victim of what we call dignity, the reverse of what the TRC public hearings were meant to do.*

When Ghana's National Reconciliation Commission began hearings in early 2003, there were some scenes reminiscent of the ones in South Africa. The victim and the victimized publicly reconciled, with great emotional impact. But there was "a feeling it was contrived. People were talking about it. . . . We stopped it," recalled Araba Sefa-Dedeh, a psychologist and the NRC's director of counseling. "If there is to be a reconciliation, it's done in private." The emphasis, she told me, was not on embracing one's former perpetrators but on "letting them go and not letting the perpetrator ruin their lives."

In spring 2003, I observed several sittings of Ghana's NRC. The hearings were held in an elegant remodeled structure that once housed the Ghanaian parliament. It is a formal setting, one that engenders solemnity. On one of the days that I attended, the commission heard the case of William Thomas Bruce. An elegant man in his sixties, Bruce wore a tailored, short-sleeve maroon shirt and carried himself with the confident air of a man accustomed to being taken seriously. His self-assurance foundered, however, as he tried to describe what had occurred on July 20, 1979. He opened his mouth, but no words came out; then he openly wept.

A mental health counselor quickly took the seat next to Bruce and whispered in his ear. Within moments, Bruce regained his composure and proceeded to tell his story. The month following the 1979 military coup led by Flight Lieutenant Jerry Rawlings, four soldiers appeared in the small restaurant Bruce owned in Accra. It was a simple place that served okra stew, rice and beans, and other local fare at what Bruce deemed to be reasonable prices. The soldiers ate happily and well. But when time came to pay the bill—which amounted to a few thousand cedis, less than three dollars U.S.—they refused to pay. The food was too expensive, they said. And they ordered Bruce outside, bundled him into a truck, and drove to a detention center.

There they proceeded to torture him. One of the soldiers produced chunks of salt and ordered Bruce to chew them. Terrified, Bruce obeyed; and as blood trickled out of his mouth, the soldier ordered him to swallow the salt. Later, after making him remove his T-shirt, they beat him with electric wires. After tiring of that, they forced him—at this point covered with blood—to chop firewood with an ax. Then they ordered him to crawl on the floor as they stomped on and beat him. "I was so weak, I couldn't feel anything," recalled Bruce. But the torture continued. They blindfolded him and ordered him to hop about while reciting, as they poked him in the chest with bayonets.

Finally, they'd had enough and took him home. His first act was to call a waitress at his restaurant to provide details on his life insurance policy along with instructions that his nephew in London should take over the business in the event of his death—which he then thought might be imminent. A few weeks later, soldiers returned and ransacked his restaurant and stole his liquor; and some weeks after that, other soldiers came; and—as he had not yet replaced his stock—they beat him for not having liquor. At no point during the ordeal were charges brought; nor was any coherent explanation ever offered as to why he had become a target. Apparently, for reasons only known to themselves, the soldiers had become annoyed with him—perhaps because, as a successful businessman, he owned things simple soldiers did not.

Later that year, one of the soldiers among the original assailants returned and ordered one glass of gin after another. At one point the inebriated soldier apologized for having tortured Bruce in July. He solicited Bruce's forgiveness and invited the restaurant owner to join him for a drink.

"No way will I have a drink with you," stammered Bruce and then asked the man what he would have done if Bruce had died. "Would you have brought the drink to my graveside?"

Bruce concluded his testimony with a tribute to the commission, thanking the commissioners for providing the opportunity for him "to make the whole of Ghana, the whole world, know what happened to me."

One of the commissioners, a former military commander, shook his head in apparent disgust. The world needs to know, he said, of "the sort of people who have been humiliated, who have been embarrassed. *People who command respect.*" He sighed. "Young boys, maltreating elders, crawling on your elbows." The commissioner's eyes turned upward, toward the spectators' gallery, and he added, "Let him [Bruce] cry, to get [out] some of the pain. . . . I hope that by the end of this morning, a lot of the pain has come out."

Another commissioner, a Catholic bishop, asked, "If that soldier came back today and offered a drink, would you accept it?"

"I would embrace him and tell him I have forgiven everything," said Bruce.

During a recess, I asked Bruce what had changed. Why was he willing to forgive the man now, but not at the time? During the months following his torture, Bruce explained, he was still suffering from the beatings. He was in considerable physical pain and was unable to raise his arms above his head. As he spoke, he raised both hands above his head. Although he did not have full mobility, he had regained much of what he had lost.

I took his answer as a way of saying that, for him, forgiveness stemmed primarily from the healing of his physical injuries. It was not the result of an intense conversation with God, or of following a complicated process of working through resentments. Nor was it the result of any particular insight into the soldiers' motives or psyche. It was simply that his suffering no longer defined his life. His physical recovery—and the passage of time— had allowed him to let go of his bitterness.

Clearly other things had happened as well. In the years since 1979, he had managed to thrive. Despite his traumatic experiences, his businesses had grown. His position in society had been strengthened; and Ghana itself had changed. He was no longer in fear of soldiers who might suddenly appear and subject him to unimaginable indignities. A sense of stability and fairness had returned. All was right, more or less, with his world. So he could afford to forgive—at least theoretically. Who knows what might become of that commitment to forgive if Bruce, like Amy, had to take it out of the realm of theory and put it into practice with a real human being who is not particularly forgivable?

While in Ghana, I reflected on a similar hearing I had attended in Peru. A man had appeared to talk about his brother who had been abducted by soldiers and had never returned. The man was in no mood to hear talk of forgiveness. So he preempted any such discussion by announcing that he had no intention of forgiving or of shaking hands with the men who kidnapped his brother. He merely wanted them to tell him what they had done with him. Clearly, the hurt was too raw and his world too unsettled for him to consider giving the gift of forgiveness to the people who had brought so much trauma to his family.

For some people, forgiveness is part of the process that helps to set their world right again. For others, it is a step that can only be taken—if at all—once a sense of normalcy and security have returned. Even the most diehard forgiveness advocates, such as Enright, do not see forgiveness as an automatic or necessarily natural development. If the injury is deep, attaining a state where one is free of resentment, where one can consider embracing one's tormentor, can be an arduous, even painful, process—which is only one of many reasons why you might ask whether certain people, certain acts, should be forgiven at all.

2.

THE UNFORGIVABLE

In *The Sunflower*, Simon Wiesenthal famously asked whether a soldier who participated in an atrocity can be forgiven—and, if so, by whom. A dying twenty-two-year-old Nazi, a member of the SS, confesses to Wiesenthal and solicits his forgiveness. Wiesenthal, imprisoned in a Nazi concentration camp, has no choice but to hear the man's confession.

The crime, which haunts the man's memory, occurred in Dnepropetrovsk, a city in the Ukraine under Nazi occupation. The soldier's unit came upon a group of perhaps two hundred Jews, and the soldiers drove them, like cattle, into a house, forcing many of them to carry cans of petrol. When the soldiers happened upon another group of Jews, they too were herded into the structure. On command, the soldiers tossed grenades into the building, which burst into flames. As the occupants died, screaming in agony, the Nazis shot anyone who tried to escape.

The soldier who summoned Wiesenthal to his deathbed had been mortally wounded in a subsequent military campaign. Those wounds had brought him to the makeshift medical center where he had prevailed upon the unwilling Wiesenthal to hear his confession: "In the long nights while I have been waiting for death, time and again I have longed to talk about it to a Jew and beg forgiveness from him."

Wiesenthal was uncertain how best to respond to such a bizarre longing and to such a morally repugnant tale. Unable to forgive the man, he ultimately opted not to respond, silently rejecting the plea for absolution. When he discussed the incident with his fellow prisoners, they supported his course of inaction. Indeed, one pointed out that forgiveness was not within his power, that no one could forgive on behalf of others.

Nonetheless, Wiesenthal could not cast the soldier out of his mind. And years later, when he was free and the war was over, he paid a visit to the man's mother. He told her that he had known her son briefly, had talked to him through the window of a hospital train, and that the son had sent greetings to her. Tempted as he was to tell the mother about the mass murder in which her son had participated, he could not "shatter her illusions about her dead son's inherent goodness."

Wiesenthal's question to his readers—one that has engaged some of the world's foremost thinkers—is: "What would you have done?" It is not a question asked with dispassion, since he frames consideration of it with the following statement: "Forgetting is something that time alone takes care of, but forgiveness is an act of volition, and only the sufferer is qualified to make the decision."

The sufferers in this particular case would seem to be the hundreds of Jews who died so horribly at the hands of the soldiers and his comrades. So Wiesenthal essentially is saying that no one is qualified to forgive the soldier's acts—except the dead, who have no voice.

In rereading Wiesenthal's essay, I found myself wondering how his principle applied to the situations of Nethercut, Khamisa, and Jaeger Lane. In each case, a perpetrator had committed the most horrible act a parent can imagine. And in each case, the parent forgave him. And yet, by Wiesenthal's standard, they were unqualified to do so—since the wrong, at least the greater wrong, had been done not to them but to their children. So what then did it mean that the parents had made journeys full of torment to arrive at a state of forgiveness? Or that Nethercut had granted forgiveness not only to the murderer but also, in a deeply symbolic ceremony, to another man who had murdered someone else's child?

If only the sufferer can forgive, or can decide to forgive, then people such as Nethercut, people who are incidental casualties to murder, can only forgive their own suffering. They can tell the killer, in essence, "I cannot forgive you for killing my child, but I can forgive the pain you have caused me." By the same token, a prisoner selected at random in a concentration camp could respond to the soldier's plea, if he were so disposed, with something along the lines of: "I cannot forgive the killing of the Jews in Dnepropetrovsk, or any other atrocity you might have committed; I can only forgive the pain that you and your comrades have forced—and continue to force—me to bear." But is the prisoner really limited to such a response? Does it make sense to say that you can forgive only an act committed against you personally?

Certainly it makes sense if we assume that forgiveness is, in some sense, the discharging of a debt. Your terrible actions have taken something of value from me. Therefore you owe me; and only I can discharge your debt. Neither my mother, my father, nor others in my ethnic or religious group—who might be, in some respects, similarly wronged—can forgive this specific debt, for it is owed to me and me alone.

But is forgiveness really about discharging a debt? I doubt that it is in most cases. That would mean that forgiveness, once extended, somehow evens the score, that it takes things back to square one—that, in terms of the cosmic ledger books at least, it returns the interested parties to a condition equivalent to the wrong never having been committed. And no one—no human, at any rate—can grant that kind of forgiveness. Such a thing would fall, if it falls anywhere, under the rubric of divine absolution. All of which raises the question again of what does it mean to forgive?

For Bruce, the tortured Ghanaian businessman, it does not mean that he is absolving his torturers of their guilt. It seems to be a resolution, an acknowledgment, a prayer that goes something like this: *I have recovered from the unjustified harm that you did me. And now that I have had a chance to tell the world my story, I will no longer spend my time hating you, or obsessing about you. I can finally let my demons go. I can finally let you go.*

For Amy, who was trying to redefine and renew the relationship with her mother, forgiveness is a somewhat more complicated matter. The kind of forgiveness to which she aspired is of a much more intimate sort. She wished to banish the bitterness and rancor; but she wished, in addition, to restore her mother to a place of affection and esteem.

For those, like Khamisa and Nethercut, struggling to comprehend the murder of a child, forgiveness amounts to saying: *I do not absolve you from the murder of my child. I have neither the power nor the desire to do such a thing. But I do commit myself to foreswear revenge and also to extend compassion.*

Compassion, not absolution, is what the young soldier in Wiesenthal's parable seemed to be seeking. He was clearly tormented by what he had done and was endeavoring to explain how he, a decent person who personally bore Jews no ill will, could have done such a horrible thing. He was seeking reassurance that a Jew could understand that he was not at heart a monster.

Wiesenthal, who was in a concentration camp and still under the soldier's dominion—and this was a soldier who had eagerly joined the Hitler Youth and, just as eagerly, volunteered for the SS—was clearly in no spiritual, emotional, or political position to show such compassion. What human being in such circumstances could? Most people, given the chance, would probably have spat in the soldier's face. Yet once the war was over and the soldier was dead, Wiesenthal felt a considerable amount of empathy for the young soldier's mother—whom he would not have sought out had he not felt some compassion for her son.

Bernard Schlink's novel, *The Reader,* also deals with the issues of compassion, absolution, and the Holocaust. In this case, the object is an older woman who seduced the protagonist when he was a fifteen-year-old student. One day she disappears without explanation; and when he next sees her, she is on trial in postwar Germany for crimes connected with the Holocaust. It turns out that when she vanished she had joined the SS and had served in concentration camps. She has been charged with selecting women to be killed and with locking women in a church and standing by as they burned to death. For those crimes—it emerges that she may not be as deeply implicated as the evidence seems to indicate; and for their own reasons, neither she nor the protagonist bring the partially exculpatory facts to light—she is condemned to life in prison. After serving eighteen years, she is scheduled for release. But rather than face the world, the woman hangs herself, leaving her money to the daughter, now grown, of a woman who survived the fire. The protagonist, now a legal scholar, duly offers the daughter the money, which she refuses. Instead, she tells him to donate it to a Jewish organization, but one not associated with the Holocaust. "Using it for something to do with the Holocaust would seem like an absolution to me, and that is something I neither wish nor care to grant," she says. For similar reasons, some Jews rejected the idea of German reparations, seeing it as an empty gesture by an unworthy nation to use their consent as a way of rebuilding Germany's good name.

Among the many things that Schlink makes clear is that the woman, while not entitled to absolution, may be worthy of compassion—and that extending compassion is very different from removing the burden of guilt.

A friend tells the story of a close relative, a Jew, who escaped from Czechoslovakia during World War II. Shortly after the war's official end, the man reentered his homeland as a member of a regiment of free Czechs under British command. The soldiers stumbled upon two SS officers and were unsure what to do with them. Shortly thereafter, a Russian soldier happened along and insisted that they execute the Nazis. My friend's relative, the sole Jew among them, objected—arguing that, formal hostilities having ceased, they had no right to execute the men but should take them prisoner. The others ignored him. They raised their weapons and executed the SS men on the spot.

Afterward, the Jewish soldier took the younger officer's identification book together with love letters the SS officer had received from his wife. He sent the items to the widow, to whom he wrote a note telling her that her husband had died bravely. Still, the incident weighed on his conscience. And a few months later, he mentioned what had happened in Czechoslovakia to a Jewish friend in London. The friend told him not to worry, that the SS were all murderers and "deserved to be executed."

The soldier reaching out to the SS man's widow was not, in my friend's view, "an act of forgiveness. . . . It was a human act" motivated by compassion and possibly also by a touch of guilt for not having intervened.

In the context of the Holocaust, such human acts of compassion toward perpetrators and their sympathizers take on a particular weight. For among the evils perpetrated in the world, the Holocaust holds a special rank.

In Geneva, Switzerland, at a preparatory conference for the United Nations Conference on Racism in 2001, Tom Lantos, the congressman and Holocaust survivor, ended up in a meeting with some people arguing the case of reparations for the enslavement of Africans and their descendants. Lantos managed to stay calm through most of the dialogue but reached a point of obvious exasperation at the suggestion that the slave trade also constituted a holocaust. There was something very distinct, he pointed out,

THE UNFORGIVABLE | 53

about the culmination of events that ended with a third of the world's Jews being "put into gas chambers and cremated." There was a "distinction in the designation." Yes, other horrible things had occurred; and, yes, those things ought to be recognized. Nothing stands in the way, he said, "of a word being created for the Cambodian nightmare or the Rwandan nightmare." But to call them—or the slave trade—by the same name as Nazi evil would be "trivializing the Holocaust."

The Holocaust was indeed a particular horror that has—and merits—a specific designation. But does that mean that the evil perpetrated in its name was a special brand of evil—or that its perpetrators and enablers are beyond the reach of comprehension or compassion?

In *The Roots of Evil,* Ervin Staub, himself a Holocaust survivor—a native of Budapest, he found safety in one of the houses of Raoul Wallenberg—argues against the tendency to "romanticize" the Holocaust to such an extent that it becomes an incomprehensible evil of "mythic proportions."

In *Still Alive,* a memoir of a childhood partially spent in Nazi concentration camps, Ruth Kluger observes: "[We] insist that their deaths were unique and must not be compared to any other losses or atrocities. Never again shall there be such a crime.

"The same thing doesn't happen twice anyway. Every event, like every human being and even every dog, is unique. . . . In our hearts we all know that some aspects of the Shoah have been repeated elsewhere, today and yesterday, and will return in a new guise tomorrow; and the camps, too, were only imitations (unique imitations, to be sure) of what had occurred the day before yesterday."

Hundreds of thousands of Armenians were murdered by Turks during the genocide of 1915–1916. That was clearly evil practiced on a grand scale. So was the so-called ethnic cleansing in Bosnia and the genocides in Rwanda and Cambodia. Indeed, mass murder and torture in countries around the globe, from Guatemala to

East Timor, have made it clear that, as awful as the Holocaust was, it did not stem from a uniquely German impulse—that Nazism in its essence reflected values not at all peculiar to post–World War II German society.

In *Into the Heart of Darkness,* South African journalist Jacques Pauw ponders the question of how South Africa's state assassins were formed: "[Did] apartheid create these monsters? Or are they simply evil? What drives one to push the barrel of a gun against somebody's head and blow his brains away? Or pull a tube over somebody's face and suffocate him while he moans and pleads: *'Asseblief, my bass, asseblief'* (please, boss, please). Or push an iron rod into somebody's anus or electrocute him with a power generator?"

What, indeed, is it that drives human beings to genocide and unspeakable atrocities? Staub has come up with a formula of sorts, beginning with cultural traits—not in the sense of German culture, Turkish culture, or Cambodian culture, but in terms of a broad set of shared cultural attributes. Societies that devalue certain groups, foster unquestioning respect for authority, and that nurture both a sense of vulnerability and superiority seem particularly susceptible to genocidal impulses. And within those societies, some types are much more susceptible than others. What types? Those who lack empathy, have a poor self-image, and are aggressive and authority oriented.

A handful of cultural and personality traits can only go so far in helping one understand why some societies and some people go so wrong. But they are perhaps the beginning of a sense of understanding—and that, in itself, as Staub acknowledges, can be something of a problem: "For some, it is preferable not to comprehend, because comprehension might lead to forgiving."

South African psychologist Pumla Gobodo-Madikizela faced precisely that dilemma in the course of her encounters with Colonel Eugene Alexander de Kock, a character known to South Africans as "Prime Evil." De Kock holds a special place in the annals of apartheid; he was its most notorious enforcer. Tons of newsprint have been devoted to the exploits of this former commander of a police counterinsurgency unit housed at a farm north of Pretoria at a place called Vlakplaas.

In his own book, *A long night's DAMAGE,* he acknowledges that murder was state policy and that he was perhaps its leading instrument. "The murder of anti-apartheid activists was part of a broad reaction against the growing resistance to apartheid. It was obvious that so-called lawful ways of suppression had failed to stem the growing opposition. We therefore felt it necessary to use unlawful means. We used secret agents to intimidate activists, to destroy their property, to plant bombs and commit arson," wrote de Kock.

In *Into the Heart of Darkness* Pauw offers this summary of de Kock's career.

In August 1996, Eugene de Kock was convicted of six murders, conspiracy to commit murder, attempted murder, kidnapping, assault, manslaughter, defeating the ends of justice, the illegal possession of arms and ammunition, and fraud.

This was, however, only a fraction of the crimes and atrocities committed by the death squad commander. He was in command of Vlakplass for eight years, during which time he was involved in the killing of about sixty-five people. During his four-and-a-half-year stint . . . in Namibia, he commanded a unit which killed hundreds of South West African People Organisation (Swapo) infiltrators and supporters. And during the early 1990s De Kock and his men became a "third force" when they flooded the townships around Johannesburg with weapons to enable Inkatha to wage civil war against the ANC. Thousands of people died during this conflict.

De Kock was the most prominent member of the counterinsurgency forces to tell his story to South Africa's Truth and

Reconciliation Commission. He, no doubt, was motivated largely by the hope of lightening his 212-year sentence; but he also claimed to feel genuine remorse.

Gobodo-Madikizela met him shortly after he testified before the TRC concerning his role in the murder of three black policemen deemed likely to become informants. They were sent off in a car loaded with explosives that was detonated by remote control. Over a period of several months and many interviews, Gobodo-Madikizela came to see de Kock as something other than the unflinching murderer he obviously was. He was also someone who apparently went out of his way to protect children in the line of fire; and he was a person of candor and conscience who seemed sincere in his apologies to survivors. He was a good man, as he saw it, following the orders of his superiors, serving the only cause he had known—not out of hatred, but duty.

Early in the process of getting to know him, Gobodo-Madikizela came upon an agitated de Kock in the prisoner interview room. He had just finished apologizing to the widows of some men whose deaths he had orchestrated. His eyes were brimming with tears and his voice quivering as he told Gobodo-Madikizela that an apology was not enough. "I wish there was a way of bringing their bodies back alive. I wish I could say, 'Here are your husbands.' "

In an effort to comfort him, she touched his hand. It was a gesture over which she later agonized, all the more so after he pointed out that the hand she had touched was his trigger hand.

"In touching de Kock's hand I had touched his leprosy, and he seemed to be telling me that, even though I did not realize it at the time, I was from now on infected with the memory of having embraced into my heart the hand that had killed, maimed, and blown up lives," wrote Gobodo-Madikizela in *A Human Being Died That Night*.

Gobodo-Madikizela is a black South African. De Kock is the worst kind of white perpetrator. And yet she felt compassion for him, all the while worrying about the moral and psychological cost of "stepping into the shoes of a murderer through empathy."

Her dilemma, in some sense, is Wiesenthal's dilemma; it is the dilemma of anyone who chooses to show compassion to those who have been the henchmen of criminal states. But ultimately, Gobodo-Madikizela concluded that de Kock was worthy of mercy. "Our capacity for such empathy is a profound gift in this brutal world," she wrote. Wiesenthal came out—intellectually, at least—on a different side, which, of course, is his prerogative. No one has an obligation to offer such a "profound gift." But one certainly has the right to, provided one is willing.

When I asked psychologist Robert Enright his reaction to Wiesenthal's question, he noted that he knew Holocaust victims "who have forgiven and benefited greatly." For others, he acknowledged, that may not be the case. He can understand those who choose not to forgive. But he would vigorously challenge a person who says that no one should forgive an SS officer. "If I'm next to them in the concentration camp and I said I would forgive, would they consider me wrong?" he asked.

Wiesenthal presumably would consider him wrong. Gobodo-Madikizela, I suspect, would not. But in the end, a soldier may not be the best example of a person who commits an unforgivable offense. For putting aside the question of who is qualified to forgive, the fact remains that soldiers, for the most part, are presumably following orders.

As de Kock self-servingly argued in his memoir: "I do not deny that I am guilty of the crimes, many of them horrible, of which I am accused. . . . But we at Vlakplass, and in the other covert units, are by no means the guiltiest of all. That dubious honor belongs to those who assembled us into the murderous force that we became, *and which we were intended to be all along.*" (Emphasis, his.)

Journalist Jeremy Gordin, in the afterword of de Kock's book, makes the point even more forcefully: "De Kock certainly believed . . . that he was fighting a war. . . . He looked upon him-

self as a soldier. . . . But—the rejoinder would be—that he nevertheless made the personal decision to kill people. Yes, he did. But
he killed those whom he was told or whom he believed were enemies of the state. He believed in what he was doing, as did his
superior officers, his society and his government."

Certainly a soldier following orders in a covert unit, or even in
a concentration camp, is different from an individual who simply
decides to commit evil acts of his own volition. Not that the soldier's actions are excusable. As the Nuremberg trials made clear,
"I was only following orders" is not a moral escape hatch. Yet,
even at Nuremberg the fact that one was following a superior's
bidding was a possible mitigating circumstance. "The fact that the
defendant acted pursuant to the order of his Government or of a
superior shall not free him from responsibility, but may be considered in mitigation of punishment if the Tribunal determines that
justice so requires," read Article 8 of the charter for Nuremberg's
international military tribunal. In their choice of those charged,
the Nuremberg prosecutors made a distinction between a lowly
SS officer following orders and someone in command.

"I selected the defendants . . . by rank . . . and by education,"
noted Benjamin Ferencz, chief prosecutor of SS extermination
troops, at a June 2003 symposium at New York's Museum of
Jewish Heritage. Ordinary soldiers were not on trial at Nuremberg,
but not because they were innocent. They were given a pass largely
because it would have been impractical to try so many people, but
also because they were acting on orders few ordinary human
beings would have the fortitude to reject. They were following a
normal human impulse to follow the mob, to conform to their
leaders' expectations.

If an example is needed of just how strong the pull of confor-
mity can be, read *Destined to Witness,* the memoir of Hans J.
Massaquoi. The mixed-race child of an African diplomat and a
white German woman, Massaquoi came of age in Nazi Germany;
and like other seventeen-year-old German boys, Massaquoi

eagerly, and rather comically, applied for military service. Only the military's brutal rejection shook him out of the fantasy of winning his countrymen's respect by becoming a good German soldier.

Being obedient and weak—and therefore unwilling to disobey immoral orders—is not exactly the same as being evil; or so, in essence, said the Nuremberg tribunal. And that lesson, unfortunately, has been taken to heart by soldiers far from the battlefields of actual war: by corporate minions following the dictates of their directors, by operatives following the lead of a political boss.

But what of wrongs that have no obvious mitigating circumstances? What of betrayals not coerced by the state but committed by private individuals for their own purposes? How does one consider those wrongs in the realm of forgiveness?

Some years ago, before the scandals of sex-offender priests burst into the headlines, I was at a dinner party with a prominent Roman Catholic cleric. At one point, discussion turned to church policy for dealing with priests who had molested children.

The cleric was adamant in making the case that the church's belief in forgiveness and redemption dictated giving priests a second chance. (He did not much focus, as I recall, on priestly confession, atonement, or penance.) I thought the argument preposterous but was unable to persuade the cleric that forgiveness did not necessitate putting innocents at risks. In light of subsequent revelations, it's clear why the cleric was so unwavering. For the church essentially had a policy of shuttling chronic sexual abusers and pedophiliac priests from one unsuspecting parish to another.

How, I wondered, would victims of such abuse tackle the question of forgiveness for their abusers? My curiosity led me to Barbara Blaine and David Clohessy, founder and executive director, respectively, of SNAP—The Survivors Network of those Abused by Priests.

Blaine, one of eight children, belonged to a devoutly religious family in Toledo, Ohio. Her "whole life," as she puts it, "was rooted in the church"—so much so that when the local priest chose her as an object of affection, the thirteen-year-old Blaine docilely went along. She questioned the relationship's propriety, but in the end she blamed herself, believing it was she who had "caused the good, holy priest to sin."

The liaison set her apart from her classmates and drained her self-esteem. Dates with boys her own age, the school musical, and other teenage rituals were forbidden—because she had to be available for him. She was seventeen when she worked up the nerve to end things; but for years, she kept the secret and held the shame inside.

More than a decade later, she stumbled across an article in *The Catholic Reporter* dealing with abusive priests. That article threw her into turmoil. "I became ill. I started perspiring . . . I decided I had to get some help."

At that point, she was living in Chicago and working at a homeless shelter, but she went back to Toledo to confront her past. Church leaders—the provincial and the bishop—assured her that they would take care of things, that they would see to it that the offending priest was dealt with.

Nothing happened. The priest continued to carry on his duties as a chaplain at a large hospital, and church officials dillydallied. They would set up a meeting, Blaine would arrange time off, and at the last minute they would cancel. Or they would promise to force the perpetrator into treatment, then do nothing.

She was bewildered and ultimately enraged. "The response of the church . . . was more devastating than the abuse itself. . . . I had assumed they would do the right thing. . . . It was devastating to come to this realization that they didn't care about me. . . . They strung me along like that for several years. . . . I came to the realization they weren't going to help me and I still needed healing."

She began calling abuse victims whose names appeared in the newspaper. Sometimes they called back. The ensuing discussions persuaded her of the need for abuse victims to share their experiences. She ran a small ad in a Catholic publication inviting victims to a meeting. Those who showed up became the core of what evolved into SNAP.

Convinced the church fathers would not act on their own, Blaine decided to shake them up. She told them that a reporter had called and that she was going to go public with the name of the perpetrator—and, oh, by the way, she was also going to talk about him on a national talk show that had her booked for an appearance in two weeks' time.

Finally, she had the church leaders' attention. They sent the priest into treatment and took away his priestly faculties. Although he could no longer celebrate Mass or hear confession, he remained a priest; and though the statute of limitations had run out, they reached a financial settlement with her. Along the way, Blaine learned that she was not the first person the priest had abused. There were "hundreds, if not thousands of us molested." And all along his superiors had known of his transgressions.

For Blaine, the resolution was less than satisfying. Because the priest had served as the chaplain at a hospital for more than ten years, he was eligible for a nice retirement. He continues to get the support of some influential Catholics, who see him as the victim, and who see to it that he gets a new car every two years. "And even today, he still holds himself out as a priest."

But Blaine did gain a new sense of self-esteem. She already had a master's degree in social work but decided to pursue a law degree. She finished law school in 1996 and, following a judicial clerkship, took a job in the Cook County public guardian's office, an agency charged with protecting abused and neglected children. She also got married.

Previously, said Blaine, she was "not good at intimacy." But nearly some thirty years after suffering abuse, she was discovering a new potential in herself. She still grieves for what she considers her lost youth, but she has "let go of my anger."

She knows that many people find it healing to offer forgiveness to perpetrators. And she says that she has forgiven hers; but she has not forgiven the inaction of his superiors, the refusal to defrock him, or the betrayal of her and her family's faith. "All the forgiveness in the world doesn't take away their responsibility to protect children."

Clohessy feels much the same. A priest in his home parish of Moberly, Missouri, molested Clohessy beginning at the age of twelve. "It was always at night—out of town on a [church-related] trip." Clohessy would awaken and "find him on top of me or fondling me."

At such times, he felt a mixture of confusion and terror. When morning came, he would repress the memories, folding them into the detritus of vaguely recalled dreams. He would tell himself nothing much had happened. And when his parents would ask about his trip, he would tell them all had been fine.

The abuse ended when he was sixteen; but it was not until 1990, more than twenty years later, that the memories broke through the repression. He told his girlfriend, now his wife, what he had experienced. Clohessy sued but found the statute of limitations had run out. He also discovered that his younger brother had been molested by the same priest. That brother, who had become a priest himself, was suspended by his diocese after being accused of abusing a student.

As for Clohessy's abuser, "I feel like I've largely forgiven him. . . . I don't feel tremendous animosity toward him." Clohessy was moved to forgive in part because he believes the priest is ill, psychologically wounded. "It is so much harder to do the same with the bishop, who presumably is not sick and wounded."

Like Amy, the woman abused by her father, both Clohessy and Blaine find forgiveness easier for the molester than for those who enabled the abuse, those with the power and responsibility to stop it who did nothing—or who, worse, conspired to protect the perpetrator while denying that anything was amiss. What their attitude says, in effect, is that it is not just the act committed that determines whether something, someone, is forgivable; issues of power and moral capacity are important as well. But their attitude also says that, in the end, forgiveness has a lot less to do with the victimizer than it does with the victimized.

Psychiatrist Paula Panzer recalls an incident some years ago when she was working at a shelter for battered women. A man intent on reconnecting with his woman grabbed Panzer as she left the shelter and, holding a gun on her, commanded, "Tell that bitch to get her ass out here." Trying to maintain control, Panzer took refuge in humor. "Which bitch?" she asked. "We have fifteen." The man, not amused, dumped on her the hot tea she was holding. "Do I forgive him?" she asked rhetorically. She is not inclined to do so. Of all the clients she has counseled for rape, she observed, not one has forgiven her rapist.

Who should be forgiven? For Solomon Schimmel, professor of Jewish education and psychology at Hebrew College in Newton, Massachusetts, the answer is clear—at least for Christians and Jews: the truly repentant sinner.

"Notwithstanding the differences in Jewish and Christian theologies of forgiveness, both traditions agree that when the offender has repented, the victim should forgive him and let him know that he has done so. From a secular perspective too, forgiveness in response to apology, remorse, and restitution has psychological and social value for offender and victim," observed Schimmel in *Wounds Not Healed by Time.*

Schimmel counsels against forgiveness for the unrepentant offender: "To give him a gift of love, notwithstanding his insistence on identifying with evil, is equivalent to not holding him responsible and accountable for what he has done, and thus to treat him as less than a morally autonomous human being."

Yet, in real life, true repentance is often impossible to judge. And some crimes are so awful, some wounds so deep, that repentance, even if sincere, doesn't heal the injury or ease the pain.

Certainly many people have forgiven horrible things—beatings, torture, the killing of children, sex abuse, neglect. There is little, it seems, that cannot be forgiven—if one is so disposed. But what *should* be forgiven? What ought one feel obliged to forgive? That is not a thing that ultimately anyone but the aggrieved party can determine.

Father, forgive them; for they know not what they do. There are souls—Khamisa and Jaeger Lane come to mind—capable of showing a mercy reminiscent of Christ, and who through the exercise of that mercy transform themselves and those they touch. But forgiveness is not an "essential, crucial, necessary component for the process of healing to go forward," concedes psychologist Ervin Staub. Mental health can be achieved with something substantially less than the process that ends up with an embrace of the one, or ones, who brought chaos into your life.

Richard Cress, in other words, is not unreasonable to proclaim: "Forgive if you must, but do not allow these insensitive people to shame it from you."

Forgiveness, in the grand sense of the word, is not always possible; and sometimes—if it means, for instance, letting pedophiles run amok—it is not even desirable. There are even reasons why one might want to hold on to anger, why one might want to explore the possibility of revenge. But there is no good reason why one would choose to live in a cage of rancor and rage.

What should be forgiven? The answer is obvious and yet endlessly elusive: whatever it takes to remove one from that cage.

3.

SWEET REVENGE

LURKING IN VIRTUALLY ALL OF US IS A BIT of a monster, a fiend who cackles—wickedly, uncontrollably—as he savors revenge. There is something exhilarating, deliciously primal, about payback. It is so much more accessible, for most of us anyway, than the impulse to forgive. It is so much easier to strike back—or to fantasize about striking back—than to shower enemies with compassion and goodwill.

The instinct, as we will call it, is older than the Bible; older than Samson, who invariably answered injury by killing—generally Philistines—often hundreds at a time. It is no doubt older than literature, and perhaps as old as man.

Greek mythology is one grand opera of vengeance: Cronus taking revenge by castrating his father, Uranus. Zeus, in turn, castrating Cronus. Medea, enraged at Jason's infidelity, killing his (their) children and also his bride. Achilles, overcome with grief at Patroclus's death on the battlefield, killing Hector and taking on all of Troy to avenge him.

What would Shakespeare be without revenge? There would be no Hamlet stalking his uncle to avenge his father; no Shylock plotting against Antonio. *If a Jew wrong a Christian, what is his humility? Revenge! If a Christian wrong a Jew, what should his sufferance be by Christian example? Why, revenge!*

And as for Hollywood: Is there a male action hero dead or alive who has not played the role of the normally peace-loving guy turned into a vengeful killer by the murder of loved ones? In *Open Range,* revenge, and a hunger for regime change, turn cattlemen Kevin Costner and Robert Duvall into merciless executioners. From Charles Bronson to Arnold Schwarzenegger to Vin Diesel, wronged men—and, increasingly, women—wreak havoc in the celluloid world in the noble name of vengeance.

But for all its literary and historical precedents, for all its visceral and commercial appeal, does vengeance deserve a place of honor in today's world? Is it a proper way to deal with the wrongs done to us—either of the moment or of the past?

The World Trade Center attack spawned widespread thoughts of revenge. Few Americans did not want to somehow strike back. It transported psychologist and scholar Solomon Schimmel to a childhood fantasy—one in which he became president of the United States, commander in chief, and ordered the nuclear annihilation of Germany. This elaborate, childhood vision was fueled by the horrors of Nazi Germany, by Schimmel's fervent if futile desire to make Germany pay for the evil it had done.

"I have not forgotten nor have I forgiven . . . what the Nazis and their collaborators did during their years in power. And whenever I read accounts of Nazi crimes, my blood boils and the childhood rage and desire for vengeance and retribution against Germans is triggered. I know, however, that the feelings, directed against an entire nation . . . are irrational and immoral," wrote Schimmel in *Wounds Not Healed by Time*. Yet to this day, he admits he has no idea what he would do if he stumbled across a Nazi war criminal. He wonders whether he could resist taking the law into his own hands—and presumably meting out some brutal form of street justice.

If Schimmel were indeed to do so, much of the world would surely understand. For many cultures are quite accepting of vengeance, even of the most vicious and personal kind. There are so-called honor killings, where people—almost always women—are murdered for supposedly besmirching, generally in a sexual way, family honor. There are cases—apparently thousands of them—where women are killed for showing up with an insufficient dowry. There are religious leaders who sanction assassination—remember Salmon Rushdie—for perceived offenses against religion.

There are also serious thinkers in the West prepared to argue the merits of revenge—perhaps not to the extent of claiming a pound of flesh, but maybe a drop or two of blood. A little vengeance, they suggest, can be a tonic for the melancholy mood.

In *Getting Even* Jeffrie Murphy, professor of law and philosophy at Arizona State University, argues that vengeance in moderation can be a good thing. And he goes on to argue that vengeance—the "infliction of suffering on a person in order to satisfy vindictive emotions or passions . . . anger, resentment, even hatred—often felt by victims toward those who have wronged them"—helps to maintain the moral order. It cranks up the moral outrage, which lands criminals in jail and keeps chaos at bay. There is "no essential conflict between revenge and justice, only a conflict between justice and excessive revenge," declared Murphy in the fall 2002 newsletter of the Canyon Institute for Advanced Studies (a Christian interdisciplinary research center of Arizona's Grand Canyon University).

Like victim advocate Richard Cress, Murphy is fed up with the pressure to forgive wrongdoing at any cost, with the forgiveness lobby's efforts to make the vengeful feel guilty. Why should you turn the other cheek? Why should you embrace those who would harm you? *Before Forgiving,* a book of essays Murphy coedited with psychologist Sharon Lamb, essentially agues that the therapeutic forgiveness movement may have gone too far too fast, that it is even advocating forgiveness that may be harmful to the forgiver.

Forgiveness, says Murphy, can "sometimes be an act of weakness and insecurity—a hasty suppression of anger and resentment when that anger and resentment are neither evil nor unhealthy but rather valuable testimony to our self-respect."

Coeditor Lamb echoes psychiatrist Paula Panzer's concern for victimized women being nudged toward forgiveness. "For women, refusing to be angry historically has kept them in a position of subordination; realizing and acting on anger has led to greater rights and freedoms," she writes. Hence, "forgiveness as an act of self-help may be in some way immoral. The act of incest, the act of rape, the act of battering is not just a personal insult, it is an insult to all women and makes it more dangerous for all women to exist in the world." She agrees that it is bad to be consumed by anger but is uncertain forgiveness is the only way to find release: "A victim might find release from anger by embracing it."

The impulse to revenge appears to be hardwired in humans, a result of our evolutionary development. It may provide substantial advantages in the struggle for self-preservation, independence, and self-respect. "If I were going to set out to oppress other people, I would surely prefer to select for my victims persons whose first response is forgiveness rather than persons whose first response is revenge," observes Murphy in *Getting Even*. And he approvingly cites philosopher Immanuel Kant: "One who makes himself into a worm cannot complain if people step on him."

"As long as there is evil in the world . . . we should not, I think, welcome a world free of resentment and other vindictive passions," concludes Murphy, who confesses that he has personally indulged in acts of revenge with some measure of satisfaction. The kind of personal revenge he alludes to, of course, is on the mild side of things: denying a ride to a colleague who offended him, refusing a luncheon invitation from another, making disparaging remarks. Though these small acts of vengeance, peaceful and proportional, are not likely to spiral into violence and heartbreak, they are emotionally satisfying nonetheless.

Some years ago, late one night, I was with a friend who was greatly annoyed with her neighbor. I no longer remember what injustice the neighbor had done her; but during the evening she worked herself into such a state that simply seething submissively was no longer an option. After we pulled into her driveway, my friend leapt from the car and headed to her neighbor's lawn, which was decorated with some elaborate arrangement of small statues, stones, and plants, as I recall.

She proceeded to methodically disassemble the display, dragging various pieces to different parts of the lawn. As she worked, her mood visibly lightened. Giggling, she invited me to join in. I opted to stay on the sidelines, watching as this normally rational woman busily rearranged her neighbor's whatnots. Demented though her actions may have been, I found it impossible not to share her giddy delight—her catharsis through revenge.

Universal though the instinct for revenge may be, it is much stronger in some of us than others. And those who have it in abundance apparently pay something of a price. They are less happy with life, for the most part, than more-forgiving souls willing to let bygones go good-bye. But, paradoxically, if you are spoiling for revenge, giving up vengefulness—the inclination to return injury for injury—for forgiveness does not seem to make much difference in terms of happiness; or so concluded researchers Michael McCullough, C. Garth Bellah, Shelley Dean Kilpatrick, and Judith L. Johnson.

Their study (titled 'Vengefulness: Relationships with Forgiveness, Rumination, Well-Being, and the Big Five") was limited in terms of time and scope. The population consisted of college students, volunteers in introductory psychology courses. And the emotional injuries on which they focused—fights with parents, sexual infidelity, rumors spread by friends—were not exactly of biblical proportion. But the results were nonetheless intriguing. The researchers "found no evidence that people who became more forgiving toward their offenders throughout the eight-week time period became any more (or less) satisfied with their lives." That finding, they concluded, "calls into question the importance of forgiving one's transgressors for promoting or restoring subjective well-being."

Being gossiped about by classmates is in no way comparable to losing a child to murder. For those dealing with life-changing trauma, no form of revenge may help to heal. Forgiveness—defined, in this case, as letting go of much of the resentment—may be their only hope for recovery. But for certain people trying to cope with certain kinds of pain, revenge is not necessarily more harmful than letting go. Indeed, it may even offer some relief.

But what kind of revenge? And at what cost? Those questions are central to *Revenge,* which details Laura Blumenfeld's efforts to even the score for the attempted murder of her father by a Palestinian militant.

David Blumenfeld, a rabbi visiting Jerusalem from America, was shot—essentially at random—in the winter of 1986. Omar, however, was not a skilled marksman. The bullet merely grazed the rabbi's skull, sparing the brain. The rabbi's daughter, Laura, was still in college; but she imagined tracking down the would-be killer. She would be the avenging angel who would find him and shake him to his senses. That fantasy persisted through the years; and more than a decade later, as a journalist for the *Washington Post,* she set off to fulfill it. But she was unsure exactly how to proceed.

"I was hoping my call for revenge would stir up . . . [a] familial call to arms." But her family was not very taken with her revenge fantasy; and she realized that, for the most part, she would have to go about it alone. She knew she could not kill the assailant. He, after all, had not murdered her father—although he had tried. Nor, she knew, was she cut out to be a killer. But simply shaking him by the collar seemed insufficient; and putting a curse on him was less than sensible.

When she learned that the assailant was already in jail serving time for the crime, her hunger for revenge was not assuaged. She sought out his family in Kalandai, the West Bank, and introduced herself as a journalist. She kept secret the facts that she was Jewish and the daughter of the rabbi Omar had shot. In time, she befriended the family. Through letters smuggled into the prison by family members, she also developed a relationship with Omar. And though she did not come clean about her identity, she acknowledged knowing the man Omar had tried to kill.

Subsequently, she drew Omar into a dialogue—about David, about the Palestinian political situation, and about violence as an instrument of change. David felt no vindictiveness toward him, she told Omar; and David respected his ideology. But the man whom he had tried to kill nonetheless had a question for him: *Would he ever use violence against anyone again?*

Omar responded that he would not. By that time, his letters had revealed Omar to be a person of sensitivity and humanity. Along the way, Laura had settled on the brand of revenge she would seek. The "revenge that I wanted was . . . one that responded to the heart of the crime. So I set myself a goal that was outsized and naïve, and most of all elusive: I wanted him to realize he was wrong."

In the book's most dramatic scene, Blumenfeld shows up at a hearing where Omar is requesting early release for medical reasons. Without revealing her identity to the three-judge panel, she demands to be heard. She tells the stunned courtroom that Omar has foresworn violence and that even David Blumenfeld, the man he tried to kill, believes it is time for Omar to go home. Then— and one can hear the music swell in the soundtrack—she reveals herself to be David's daughter. She confronts Omar directly and reminds him of his promise never to resort to violence. Laura's mother, who has accompanied her to the hearing, is overcome with emotion. She declares that she forgives Omar, which horrifies her daughter.

"This was not about forgiveness," writes Blumenfeld. "I was not forgiving him. Didn't she understand? This was my *revenge.*"

In May 2003, I attended a lecture by David Blumenfeld in a synagogue in Staten Island during which he talked about his daughter's book. "Turn the other cheek is unrealistic in real life," he declared at one point. "It's great if you can do it, I guess. . . . The Jew doesn't turn the other cheek. The Jew protects himself." Still, Blumenfeld, as I had expected, steered away from endorsing an eye for an eye. "If a person hurts you, take that hurt and focus on what has been done to you . . . but not on the other person. . . . Use it constructively to counter what he tried to do. . . . I will build Israel. . . . I will visit, again and again, fearlessly. That is my form of revenge. . . . I want to see constructive revenge . . . transformative revenge."

The rabbi told a story about an elderly woman, a Holocaust survivor who was now a person of considerable wealth. Every Wednesday, she visited New York's Rikers Island prison to spend time with the inmates. During the course of those visits, through sharing her time, experiences, and her hard-nosed empathy, she managed to transform some "hardened criminal types" into more compassionate men.

Revenge as transformation. An appealing, even inspiring, concept. Yet like Laura Blumenfeld's mother, I had difficulty distinguishing between that type of revenge and what other people called forgiveness and reconciliation. The Blumenfelds had not merely let go of their bitterness, they had embraced the transgressor—and helped him to transform. *Is that really revenge?*

They certainly had not met Murphy's criteria of inflicting "suffering" in order to satisfy a vindictive lust. Perhaps, if you were willing to be linguistically flexible, you could say Blumenfeld met the definition proffered by McCullough and his colleagues: "an attempt to redress an interpersonal offense by voluntarily committing an aggressive action against the perceived offender." Blumenfeld *had* taken aggressive action; but it seemed more *for* than *against* the offender. Blumenfeld herself called it a "third way," revenge that destroyed neither oneself nor one's enemy.

Perhaps it was revenge in a broader, more biblical sense. *If your enemy is hungry, give him bread to eat; and if he is thirsty, give him water to drink; for you will heap live coals on his head, and the Lord will reward you* (Proverbs, 25: 21–22). One could read that passage, Solomon Schimmel explains, as a promise of Divine revenge. Paul "looks for the day when God will avenge. In fact, he might even understand the heaping of live coals on the head not as a sign of contrition, but of the pain, shame, and humiliation that the enemy will experience when God eventually punishes him," writes Schimmel in *Wounds Not Healed by Time*. Or perhaps, as Schimmel also insinuates, one can define revenge along the lines of Abraham Lincoln, who is reputed to have said, "I destroy my enemies when I make them my friends." For David Blumenfeld, it was apparently enough that Omar, as he put it, now "knows the answer isn't terrorism."

Revenge as transformation. Laura Blumenfeld had not just delivered Omar from terrorism; she had also vanquished her own dark impulses, and thereby avoided entering the cycle in which hate meets hate and violence spawns violence. For the danger of revenge is that it will escalate and become self-perpetuating. Or as David Blumenfeld noted in his talk, "It will never disappear." Transformation as an alternative is an appealing idea. And I will return to that in due course.

But revenge is not necessarily uncontrollable. What of more measured revenge? Not just the types that Murphy describes—snubbing a colleague, or lashing out with wit—but serious revenge, Old Testament revenge. Revenge agreed to by society, carried out by the state, need not escalate—even if that revenge means killing. But is that a kind of revenge that makes sense? It arguably might, if the death of someone who unjustifiably took someone's life is somehow essential to societal order. Or perhaps even if it simply erases some of the pain and allows survivors to get on with their lives. In such a circumstance, it could conceivably be a healthy choice, if not exactly a pleasant one to contemplate.

The place for reflecting on such issues, I decided, was Texas—
the state that executes more people, by far, than any other state.
Between 1976—when a Supreme Court decision ended the
national death penalty moratorium—and August 2003, Texas put
309 people to death, according to Amnesty International. The dis-
tant second was Virginia, with 89 executions.

In Houston, I interviewed Janice Brown. And as I found out
during our hours together, nothing about her life, or her beliefs,
was simple.

Brown is a short, heavyset woman with a direct, almost gruff,
manner. Her dark hair is sprinkled with gray and frames an
attractive, expressive face. She was born in San Diego shortly after
the end of World War II. Her parents' wartime aerospace jobs
ended with the fighting, and the family moved—to Browning,
Missouri, for seven years, then to Abbeville, Louisiana.

Her childhood was one long saga of abuse. Her mother had a
sharp tongue and a hot temper and would routinely lash out at
Janice, both verbally and physically. Terrified of her mother,
Janice at times feared she might die at her mother's hands. But it
was a male relative somewhat older than Janice who destroyed
any possibility of childhood innocence. The sexual abuse began
when she was eight and continued into adulthood.

"He told me if mother ever found out, he would kill me,"
Janice recalled. But frightened as she was of Daemon, as we will
call him, she was even more frightened of her mom, whom she
believed quite capable of murdering her if she found out what she
and Daemon were doing. So she kept the secret and lived with the
abuse. As a teenager, she would routinely take five or six baths a
day. "I was just trying to get him off of me. . . . I felt dirty all the
time." Family members thought the practice so cute that they
nicknamed her Waterbaby.

The move to Lake Charles, Louisiana, when Janice was twelve,
did not bring the abuse to a halt. "It just slowed it down." Even
Daemon's marriage didn't make him stop. During his honeymoon,

while Janice's mother took his new wife to the hospital, he cornered her in the house. "Guess what he did," she said with a grimace.

Around that time, her last year of high school, a family friend noticed that she seemed troubled. She was drinking and apparently depressed; and through the friend's intervention, Janice ended up in the Lake Charles Charity Hospital psychiatric outpatient clinic. Over a series of sessions, a therapist won her trust; and she eventually told him of the sexual abuse.

The week after she told him, her mother was summoned for a meeting with the therapist. Janice waited in the hall. When her mother emerged, she said nothing. Instead, they simply headed home, where Mom disappeared into another room, told her husband of the conversation, and called Janice's grandfather. Janice, who could hear through the door, listened as the two plotted Daemon's murder. They would lure him to the grandfather's home in Abbeville, where they would kill him.

"I remember being appalled and shocked," said Janice. She imagined returning home the next day to find Daemon had been killed and police cars parked around her house. Everyone, she imagined, would know her mother and grandfather were murderers—a stigma she believed would follow her forever. To her relief, the next day came and passed just like any other. They spared Daemon, she surmises, out of concern for his wife and child.

Those years of abuse from Daemon and her mother gave her a frightening glimpse of what the future might hold. She swore never to abuse her children "if I had children." When she did marry, at the age of nineteen, she had two children in rapid succession. "I did abuse my children," she tearfully confesses, "probably only about half as much as I was abused. " But it was still way too much, she acknowledges. She physically abused her son and daughter. And she would willingly inflict emotional pain, denying permission or approval, just because she assumed that was what parents were supposed to do.

She soon realized her first marriage was a mistake; but it nonetheless lasted some five years. It was the second marriage that, in her mind, gave her another chance at life—and at being a parent.

Doctors had told her she would never again become pregnant. She had accepted that as fate, all the more so since she realized she had not been an ideal parent. Though it was clear her husband wanted another child, he had adopted her children from her previous marriage and had never complained that he had none of his own. But one day, when he accidentally brushed against her breast, she realized her body was changing, and she knew the doctors had been wrong. Through some unforeseen "miracle," as she calls it, there was the possibility of a child.

Still, there were serious medical obstacles—including endometriosis and an incorrectly positioned uterus. So she spent Mother's Day weekend, 1977, undergoing procedures that, if all went less than perfectly, would end with the death of her unborn child. Against all odds, the fetus survived.

Janice resolved again to put aside her abusive ways. The resolution took hold. Not only was she better prepared for her new baby, but her existing children, as she put it, also "got a better mother."

Kandy was born November 22, 1977. And Janice immediately understood that she was something special. "I knew I was in the presence of something very different than I had ever seen before." In Kandy, she saw "an old soul," an intuitive wisdom that could help Janice in her world.

The child was three months old when the family moved to Houston—"from the Deep South to the Wild West," as Janice describes the move that was, in so many ways, a new beginning.

No longer was she in the orbit of her controlling mother or the repugnant Daemon. "Once I left Louisiana, as far as I was concerned he was dead." Houston also exposed her to cosmopolitan views she had not encountered in Abbeville or Lake Charles. She read voraciously to feed her hunger for spiritual sustenance, and she befriended people of various backgrounds and beliefs. She had already begun to question what she saw as the rigidity of her Southern Baptist faith; and her reading and new relationships opened her mind to other possibilities.

A year and a half after Kandy's birth, Jody was born. In time, Janice and her husband—a devout Southern Baptist—drifted apart. As her marriage broke up, she thought of the story of Solomon and of his command to split a child between two women. She resolved not to fight for custody. She also knew that although she and her husband were divorcing, he still loved her—and would not stand in the way of her being fully involved in her children's lives. In the back of her mind, there was also the fear of how she would adjust following the divorce. After divorcing her first husband, she had begun drinking heavily and had become abusive to her children. "There was a lot of anger in me. I took it out on them." She did not want to risk that happening again.

By 1987, her husband had remarried, but Janice remained a key presence in their lives. Just before Mother's Day weekend, she called and asked whether the children could spend part of that weekend with her. Though she had them on alternate weekends, Mother's Day did not fall in her week. Later she realized the divorce decree gave her the right to keep them on Mother's Day weekend irrespective of where it fell on the schedule.

Her ex-husband agreed to the request, provided that she get the children to choir practice that Saturday. She also floated the idea of the kids coming to live with her permanently at some point soon and took his reply—"We'll see"—to mean he would try to work that out.

That Friday evening Janice and the two children had dinner at a Mexican restaurant. Afterward they picked up the *Sound of Music* video. During the evening, as the video played, with Jody on the love seat and Kandy sprawled on the sofa, Janice found herself staring at Kandy. She was a beauty—slim, with brown hair and a glowing smile; but for some reason the particular focus of Janice's attention was Kandy's feet. She recalls trying to commit their contours to memory.

The next morning Kandy seemed a bit despondent and reluctant to leave. She was slow getting her things together—so much so that they arrived nearly thirty minutes late to choir rehearsal. The late arrival set off an argument with the ex-husband and angered the new wife—apparently not just at Janice but at Kandy.

The next Tuesday, around 8 P.M., Janice got home in time to hear the end of a message left by her ex-husband. "Kandy is missing and they suspect foul play," he told her when she returned the call. He advised her she should stay at home, that there was a chance Kandy was headed in her direction. "They think she left with somebody and asked him to take her to you."

The wait stretched into days. Meanwhile Janice learned the hard lesson that, as the noncustodial parent, she was a primary suspect in her daughter's disappearance. Janice and Kandy's father and stepmother were all asked to take lie-detector tests. Janice was so emotionally distressed that she flunked. "The results indicate deceit," the agent told her.

Ten days after Kandy disappeared, a distraught Janice called the FBI. "What can I do to help find my daughter?" she asked. "You can't do anything," the agent replied. "You're still a suspect." Not sure what else to do, she demanded they arrest her. Although they admitted that they were "thinking about it," they did not.

Kandy's body was found May 26, exactly two weeks after she had disappeared. The previous Friday a man walking in the wooded area had noticed an unpleasant smell and assumed it was a dead animal. When he returned that Tuesday, the smell was even stronger. When he investigated, he found a body covered with brush. Only Kandy's feet with her new white tennis shoes were visible. Her hands were bound with electrical cord and she had been shot in the head.

Several days later, Kandy's body was released to the funeral home. Janice insisted on seeing her daughter's body, although it was still in the body bag, "I can deal with things I can see," she told herself. But she was in no way prepared for what she saw. Kandy's body was badly decomposed and filled with maggots: a nightmare image that would haunt her mother for months to come.

The same day police found Kandy's body, they arrested James Otto Earhart, asleep in his car outside of Sam Houston National Forest. The obese junk dealer had visited Kandy's home the week before she disappeared. He had come in response to an advertisement for a paint sprayer. The wife had been so alarmed by his unkempt appearance that she had refused to let him into the house.

The morning of May 12, Earhart had approached another family in the neighborhood complex, expressing interest in a kitten they had advertised. It was for his daughter, he told them; it was later revealed that he had no daughter. He looked at the neighbor's daughter with such intense interest that the mother had grown alarmed and temporarily left town with her daughter.

Earhart returned to the complex that afternoon and found no one at Kandy's home. He asked a neighbor when the family was likely to return and apparently waited for Kandy to come. When the school bus dropped her off, she was wearing turquoise shorts and a white shirt. That was the last time any of the neighbors saw her alive. When the parents returned later that day, they found Kandy's backpack on the porch, her keys on the stove and the door open.

"I became suicidal after she was killed, seriously suicidal," Janice recalled. She planned to wait until her son was back in school that fall and then drive into a deserted nearby garage and leave the engine running. "I asked Jody if it was okay if I died. . . . The pain was so intense I couldn't find anything to do about it."

All the while, she was tormented by the image of Kandy in the body bag. Her pastor was little comfort; he would simply tell her that it was time for her to get on with her life. Finally, with the help of biofeedback exercises, she managed to substitute a different mental picture of Kandy. Instead of lying, maggot eaten, in the body bag on the funeral home's sterile stainless steel table, Kandy was in bed, peacefully listening to a relaxation tape that she liked.

Exactly a year after Kandy disappeared, Earhart's trial began. There was testimony about the .22-caliber gun in his car and the blood found on his clothes. It also came out that he routinely ate out of a Dumpster and still lived with his mother at the age of forty-four. A psychiatrist testified that he was not legally insane but was out of touch with reality and had deep "feelings of inadequacy and inferiority."

On May 18, 1988, the jury found Earhart guilty of murder. During a separate punishment hearing the next day, during which Earhart's sister testified that he at one point had tried to strangle her, Earhart was sentenced to death.

Trying to make sense of Kandy's short life, Janice comforted herself with the thought that Kandy had come to earth with a mission. She imagined her waiting to be born and telling her mother, "I'll come down and help you. . . . And I'll go in a way to continue to make an impact. And you'll have to deal with what I leave behind."

Part of what she left behind was an uncontainable pain. "I hated what he did, hated that Kandy was dead. Still do."

The road back to a semblance of normalcy was littered with painful reminders of the past. "It took years before killing myself was not an option," said Janice, who as part of her recovery undertook the study of trauma. It helped her to understand that folks suffering from traumatic stress "do things that violate your values. . . . That helped me become more accepting of everything on the planet."

She yearned for a chance to talk to Earhart, to ask why he had killed her little girl. But she found out that in order to do so, he would have to give her permission to visit; he had control over who was on his approved visitors list. And she could not abide the thought of giving him control over any facet of her life. She also resented the fact that he, as she saw it, was being coddled while she "was having a really tough time. Nobody was taking care of me. . . . There was *nothing* for me. And it was all about him."

Meanwhile, Earhart worked through the appeals process. He had an execution date set for 1995 but managed to get a last-minute reprieve. By August 1999 his options had run out. "I really didn't want to see him die," said Janice. She worried that the whole affair could turn into a circus, with protestors demonstrating and reporters swarming and the whole thing becoming a garish spectacle. But the fact that several other executions were scheduled around the same date, she reasoned, might dilute the attention from Earhart's. Also, her two older children were adamant about attending; and she didn't want them to go by themselves.

Earhart made no final statement. He died on August 11 at 6:24 P.M., ten minutes after poison began coursing through his body.

After seeing him die, "I began to heal," said Janice. She quickly corrected herself. "I began to heal before that," she says; but seeing Earhart die was nonetheless an important part of the process. "It had always felt like there was an attachment between me and him. And I felt that attachment break off, this rope just fell away." During all the years of his imprisonment and appeals, "I felt just as imprisoned as he was because everything was about him. I had no say over anything. . . . I was terrified that one of his appeals would work—not that I wanted him to die, but I was terrified of having to live through another trial."

"I am not a card carrier," said Janice, referring to the pro–death penalty lobby. Indeed, she is adamantly opposed to the death penalty. She's not "arrogant enough to think that for my happiness, my well-being, somebody has to die. But I will confess to being a beneficiary of the death penalty. . . . I'm sorry he had to die; but I don't take any responsibility for his death. . . . And I'm absolutely glad he's dead and I don't have to deal with him anymore."

Since he never took responsibility for Kandy's murder and continued the appeals process up to the time of his scheduled execution, Janice was unable to talk with Earhart through Texas's Victim Offender Mediated Dialogue process. But following his execution, she went through mediation with a surrogate, with someone who had killed someone else's child. Unlike Richard Nethercut, she was not interested in forgiving her child's killer by proxy. Earhart was already dead by this time. Since her surrogate had stated that he would kill again, she was more interested in showing him how much pain his action had caused.

Her surrogate, along with a buddy, had murdered someone during a carjacking. Janice hoped by bearing witness to the agony she had endured, she could engender some empathy in him and perhaps spark a transformation. If she could get him to consider the consequences of his actions, perhaps someone else would be spared from going through what she had gone through. It was a deeply emotional experience for both of them. She talked about Kandy's murder and the unbearable pain it had caused.

Then she listened to his story. He told a woeful tale of a dad so abusive that he went to sleep dreaming of ways to murder his own father. "How could he not kill somebody?" Janice wondered. "This boy started shaking as he told me his story." At the end of the day he said that he would never kill again. A large part of the reason he reached that turning point, feels Janice, is that he finally had a chance to tell his own story. "Guess how you heal," she said rhetorically. "By telling your story until you don't have a reaction to it anymore."

For her, the experience was also unexpectedly therapeutic. What she did not realize until the next day was that for her "the murder was healed. It was over. I left murder at the Wynne Unit in Huntsville."

"I was raised on a farm," said Janice. "If a dog kills a chicken, you kill the dog or give it to someone who doesn't have chickens." No one would ever think of trying to reform or transform a dog. But her mediation session had taught her something about the power of transformation. She has since become a volunteer in the Victim Offender Mediated Dialogue (VOMD) program offered by the victim services division of the Texas Department of Criminal Justice. She also joined Bridges to Life, the faith-based program that brings victims and offenders together with the objective of promoting healing for the victims and transformation for the victimizers. For Janice, going into prisons as a Bridges volunteer has been and still is a large part of her recovery—"a wonderfully healing experience."

Knowing that I would ask the question, said Janice, she had called her two oldest children and asked them how Earhart's death had affected them. For her son John, she said, it was quite simple. "I don't hate him anymore," John had said. "I hated him. Once he was dead, I didn't hate him anymore."

For Angel, it was "the last chapter of that book. . . . I was so angry. He killed my sister. I was *so* angry."

"Angel, you're *still* angry," Janice had told her. But that anger is something that Janice more than understands. "He robbed her of a sister, who was very precious, but he also robbed her of being able to bring up memories." Every memory she had of her sister is now polluted with thoughts of Earhart.

Janice's own feelings about Earhart lean toward the sorrowful. She had this dream that he might transform himself in prison—in the manner, perhaps, of Karla Faye Tucker, who murdered a couple with a pickax in 1983 but became a born-again Christian—and sparked a national debate on clemency, rehabilitation, and the death penalty—before her execution in Texas in 1998. "I wanted Earhart to do that . . . to make his life amount to something. . . . That would have been the gift he could have given me and Kandy. It wasn't to be."

As for Daemon, there was also a reckoning of sorts. In 2002 he called and teased her in the manner of an old boyfriend. "Remember me?" he playfully asked. Janice refused to play along. "I told him that I remembered very well." She then proceeded to lecture him on how he had ruined a good part of her life. As she scolded and reminded him of exactly what he had done, he started to cry. He also asked her to forgive him.

"Never in all those years had forgiveness come up. . . . I wasn't going to let him off the hook. . . . I wanted him to sweat it out a bit," she recalled. So she made him wait a week for the answer, at which point she called and told him that she forgave him. Then she added that she would never talk to him again unless he told his wife what he had done. Daemon mumbled something and quickly got off the phone. He, again, was out of her life.

Has she truly forgiven him? Did she forgive Earhart? "You can only forgive somebody against whom you hold a grudge. If I hold a grudge against you, it would be my job to forgive you." But she held no grudge against Daemon or Earhart, she explained, making forgiveness irrelevant.

I was intrigued by Janice's story for many reasons. Her pain, her struggle, her journey had led her in so many directions. Forgiveness, retribution, transformation. She had sampled them all. Forgiveness, of a sort, for the sexually abusive relative who had tormented her so much of her life. Revenge, carried out by the state, for the life of her daughter. Attempted transformation of those prisoners with whom she shared her story and from whom she drew a bit of sustenance—and who, unlike Earhart, were motivated to change. Janice's story was a reminder of how messy real life can be; of how simple single answers to deep pain or major life problems are almost always inadequate. But what particularly struck me about Janice's experience was how little revenge meant in the end. She was not really interested in revenge. And when the state insisted on taking it on her behalf, it brought no joy. It was only a means of release—a way, finally, of uncoupling her life from that of the man who had brutally murdered her daughter. Her story, in that respect, was much like Paula Kurland's.

Kurland is another Bridges to Life volunteer who lost a daughter to murder. September 13, 1986, was Mitzi's twenty-first birthday. It was also the day she died.

The killer, twenty-six-year-old Jonathan Wayne Nobles, had been stalking Mitzi's roommate. Strung out on drugs and alcohol, he broke into their Austin, Texas, apartment. Mitzi awakened to her roommate's screams and rushed to investigate. Nobles stabbed the roommate fourteen times, killing her, and stabbed Mitzi twenty-eight times. Mitzi's boyfriend tried to intervene and Nobles repeatedly stabbed him as well. The boyfriend lost an eye but survived. Mitzi did not. She "bled to death in the corner of a closet in the fetal position," said Kurland.

Nobles accidentally stabbed himself during the commotion and left blood at the scene. When the police came for him six days later, he confessed to the crime. He was convicted of the murders and sentenced to death in October 1987.

Kurland, a plainspoken woman who works in sales, wanted desperately for Nobles to pay for his crime. She even took a less demanding job so she could stay on top of the appeals process—and do anything she could to block his pleas for leniency. When Nobles applied to be an organ donor, Kurland was appalled—seeing it as a ploy for him to avoid execution in the death house, since the organs could only be preserved if he was killed in a less conventional manner. The state refused his request. "Thank God for that," said Kurland.

Despite her determination to see him dead—"I wanted my face to be the last face he saw on this earth"—she also wanted to confront him while he was living; but at that time Texas did not allow death row inmates to participate in the victim offender mediation program. The rules changed in 1998, the year Nobles was scheduled to die, and Kurland became the first family survivor to go though mediation with someone on death row.

On the appointed day—September 22, 1998—Kurland received communion from the priest. She was stunned to learn a short time later that Nobles had converted to Catholicism and had received communion from the same priest. *He already took my daughter; now he has taken my religion* flashed through her mind.

Kurland had expected a very short session, one in which she would, in effect, tell Nobles off for taking such a precious life. "I wanted to let him know how I felt. I didn't care how he felt."

The encounter went on for nearly six hours, and Kurland found it surprisingly cathartic. "The mediation gave me back my life. I walked out of there a new person because I was able to say everything back to him, and he accepted it. . . . Mediation was, for me, a new beginning."

The execution took place, October 7, 1998, two weeks after that mediation session. Thanks, in part, to their meeting, Kurland's feeling had softened somewhat toward him; but even though she had forgiven him—her church, she believed, demanded that of her—she still felt he had to die. "You couldn't pretend [the murders] didn't happen just because forgiveness happened." She also felt that if he were ever freed, Nobles would surely kill again: "Jonathan was a dangerous person."

His death, which Kurland witnessed, was "a very sad situation, but also a healing situation. . . . It was as if I had been bound and all of that had been cut loose. . . . It's not a pleasant thing to watch. I don't want to do it again; but it was the only thing that could break that chain.

"Jonathan was the focal point of my life for years," she said. After his death, "I was able to be a mom again, able to be a grandmother, able to be a human being." Before his death, she had always felt like there was "a huge weight, waiting to crash down." Finally she was free not only from Nobles, but "also free from other things that had happened in my life" and free "to ask forgiveness of people I have hurt."

Execution, of course, is the most extreme measure the state can

take, the ultimate revenge, or retribution, on behalf of those grievously wronged—in the name of those who, being dead, cannot
revenge themselves. To the extent that survivors stand in for those
murdered loved ones, the state takes revenge on their behalf as
well. But not every survivor relishes such revenge.

The sister of John Sage, the Bridges to Life founder, was brutally murdered in 1993. She was stabbed in the throat as she
begged for her life, battered with a statuette, and suffocated with
a plastic bag. The assailants—one man, one woman—were
caught shortly thereafter and sent to death row. The man died of
AIDS while awaiting execution. The woman has been appealing
the sentence. At one point, when an appeal was denied, Sage took
a call from a producer for a national television program; the producer was interested in talking to someone spoiling for revenge,
someone who would say, in effect, how great it was the perpetrator was to be killed.

Sage could not summon up the expected rage mixed in with
euphoria at the woman's impending death. "I realized that I'm
not bitter, not angry," said Sage. "It's not eating at me like it
was. . . . When you get to a point it's not eating at you, you don't
want revenge. . . . She got the death sentence. I'm not excited
about it."

Even though Connie Hilton's perpetrators dragged her through
hell she, likewise, refuses to make revenge the focus of her existence. In 1990, shortly after Hilton and her husband had settled
into their new country home, three armed intruders broke in.
They killed her husband and dog and they raped and viciously
beat Hilton, leaving her for dead. Only one of the assailants was
caught; and he received the death penalty. We spoke in June 2003,
shortly after she had received the phone call telling her an execution date had been set. "When I got the phone call . . . part of me
was relieved, part of me was extremely sad, not for him, for his
family; because he made such a stupid mistake," said Hilton. At
one point, she felt so much rage, Hilton confided, that she thought

she personally could put the needle in his arm. "Right now, I don't even want to watch it. I don't want him dead anymore. I just don't want him hurting anybody else." Nonetheless, she said, she would probably attend the execution because certain family members were adamant about going. "I have to be there to support them." She did have one concern about the execution, one she had only recently realized.

"One thing that scares me . . . I feel after the execution, I feel maybe it will be my turn." For so many years she had been strong for her family; she had been the caretaker, helping everyone get through the aftermath of the horrible ordeal. After the execution, she feared, something inside of her might just give out.

What does witnessing an execution do for the mental health and emotional well-being of survivors? For some it brings relief; for others grief or disappointment. It is virtually unexplored territory in the social science literature, and whether it helps most people get on with their daily lives remains an open question.

In May 2000, Robert Anthony Phillips, a reporter for the website APBnews.com, published a report based largely on interviews with survivors. One who witnessed the execution of a serial killer who had murdered his twin sister described his euphoric reaction: "I said, 'Die you monster. Yes! . . . I felt like a ton of bricks had been lifted off my back. The power slammed into him and he jerked as much as he could and that was it. I saw the life going out of his hands. Afterward, me and my brothers smoked cigars to celebrate."

In the same article Phillips quotes Gail Leland, founder of the National Coalition of Homicide Survivors, who notes that many family members become depressed after an execution. Execution, after all, does not bring the loved one back. The agony of absence remains—which is something well understood by people who have lost a loved one.

Azim Khamisa sent me a video of him addressing a group of schoolchildren. At one point he movingly, rhetorically, asks,

"Would revenge bring my son back to me? . . . Would revenge stop the pain and the hurt that we feel?" The children, as one, shout, "No."

Whatever benefits might accrue from witnessing an execution, the vast majority of homicide survivors will not have that privilege—for the simple reason that most murderers are not executed. Even in Texas, aggressive as it is in seeking the death penalty, only a fraction of murderers actually take the walk to the death house. Between 1988 and 2001, the number of murders per year reported in Texas ranged from a low of 1,236 to a high of 2,651. During those same years, the number of executions per year ranged from 3 to 40. However one looks at those figures, a lot of people are escaping the needle. There is a clear element of capriciousness in who actually ends up executed. And even for those who do end up killed by the state, the process is so long and draining that by the time the day of death comes around revenge fantasies have often faded.

Mary Miller, of Families & Friends of Violent Crime Victims in Washington State, told me she no longer even advises survivors to fight for the death penalty. "There have been only four people executed here since 1981 when the death penalty was reinstated, three of whom refused to appeal," she pointed out in early 2003. "Currently we have ten people on death row—the oldest dating to 1991. Washington is under the jurisdiction of the Ninth Circuit Court of Appeals, probably the most anti–death penalty court in the nation." Her point was that, as a practical option, the death penalty was essentially an illusion, at least in Washington State— and that it made little sense for survivors to invest their energies fighting for it. They may be better off, she figures, simply settling for seeing the perpetrator in jail.

In Texas, those intent on ensuring a murderer is never again allowed on the street have no option but the death penalty, since legislators there have taken life without the possibility of parole off the table—out of fear, apparently, of an outbreak of mercy if that option becomes available. Anyone convicted of a capital crime is eligible for parole after forty years. "Opponents of this measure claim that offering a jury this option will decrease the number of times the death penalty is handed down. This may be true, but life in a Texas prison is certainly not easy. Texas is a world leader in executions, and we are in little danger of appearing to be anything but tough on crime," argued State Senator Rodney Ellis, who was proposing the option of a life sentence without the possibility of parole.

But even if the process were more efficient, less capricious, more predictable, and speedier—and given the real possibility of error, and the state's need, through the appeals process, to lessen the possibility of the wrongly convicted being put to death, it's hard to see how it could be—does revenge, of the ultimate sort, make any real sense?

There are, after all, criminals who want to die. What kind of revenge is it to take their lives? Isn't the point of revenge to make people suffer, to force them to take punishment they don't want? And even for those who go kicking and screaming to their deaths, is revenge ever truly complete? The taste of revenge is inevitably bittersweet. When the injury is as huge as the loss of a loved one, what amount of suffering by the perpetrators will suffice? How does one equate a relatively pristine execution with being raped, knifed, battered, choked, and drowned? With being terrorized in one's own home? With being forced to beg for one's life? Would hanging the perpetrator by his toes and slowly slicing him to death suffice? Or would burying him in hot sand leaving him to wild beasts do? And if we could somehow get the calculus right, what civilized state could carry out the torture?

And what of those who find salvation? Who manage to transform themselves into worthwhile, even holy, human beings? Does not that transformation take the soul—and some of the point—out of revenge? For if part of the point of revenge is to return injury for injury, to make the damned suffer their sins, what is the point of sending them to Paradise?

One is reminded of Hamlet's dilemma. As he is poised to kill Claudius, he realizes Claudius is praying—and that there is the possibility that, in killing him, he will do him a favor.

> *A villain kills my father; and for that,*
> *I, his sole son, do this same villain send*
> *To heaven.*
> *Why, this is hire and salary, not revenge.*

For every survivor who responds to an execution with a shouted, "Hallelujah! The wicked beast is dead," there seems another who wonders why the pain won't stop, who knows that nothing that anyone could do to a perpetrator will make up for what has already been lost. Revenge may be one of the oldest impulses around, but it doesn't always lead people to a state of peace. And revenge—at least of the ultimate kind—raises questions not easy to dismiss.

If we grant the difficulty in forgiving for wrong done to another, how does one revenge on another's behalf? If you kill my daughter, is it you that I should kill, or is it your daughter I should take? It is at least an arguable proposition that I cannot ethically avenge a wrong I did not suffer. If you did not kill me, how do I dare kill you? If I really believe in an eye for an eye, should I not kill someone close to you—to at least make you suffer what I have suffered? But certainly the state cannot stand by as I kill innocents—or even the guilty, for that matter—to satisfy my lust for revenge. And if the instrument of my revenge is the state, no state can justify killing those who have done no harm themselves in order to satisfy the need for equivalence in revenge. Indeed, the larger question is, "Should the state be involved at all in killing to satisfy the personal need for revenge?"

Author-attorney Scott Turow believes the answer is no. "Once we make the well-being of victims our central concern and assume that execution will bring them the greatest solace, we have no principled way to grant one family this relief and deny it to another. From each victim's perspective, his loss, her anger, and the comfort each victim may draw from seeing the killer die are the same whether her loved one perished at the hands of the Beltway Sniper or died in an impulsive shooting in the course of a liquor store holdup," writes Turow in *Ultimate Punishment*.

One can argue, of course, that the state does not have to satisfy each individual need for relief; it need only make clear that certain acts are likely to carry grave consequences—and that the state will not take revenge on every deserving soul, but on a symbolic few. One can also attempt to distinguish state retribution from revenge.

"Retribution, with its advertised virtues of measured proportionality, cool detachment, and consistency is contrasted with vengeance—the voice of the other, the primitive, the savage call of unreason. . . . Vengeance must be kept at bay, so the argument goes, because it represents an unwarranted concession to an anger and passion that knows no limits," observed Austin Sarat in an essay included in *Breaking the Cycles of Hatred*.

Sarat ultimately rejects the idea of measured proportionality. When it comes to killing criminals, he argues, there is not much of a difference between revenge and retribution. Indeed, he sees the increasing tendency to give weight to victims in capital trials as part of a disturbing trend. "Throughout the West there is today a nagging doubt that public processes can be built on anything but rage and grief. That is what the call to hear the voice of the victim signals; that is what the return of revenge suggests," writes Sarat in *When the State Kills*.

One can easily argue the question either way—which is one of the reasons debates on the death penalty tend to end up where they began, with parties holding tighter than ever to whatever views they brought to the table.

I happen to think executing people is a fundamentally bad idea—and a terribly inefficient use of resources. I think it hopelessly confuses public and private agendas. And it invites fatal mistakes that can never be corrected. I won't even bother to voice the moral objections, which are myriad. But I will concede that for some survivors of homicide victims, executions can provide a much-deserved sense of release. It allows them, in witnessing the ending of one life, to get on, in some sense, with their own. For them, revenge is possibly healthy—though the question remains of whether that need for release can be met in some better way. And revenge is probably even healthier in its nonfatal doses—ruining a neighbor's lawn display, refusing a colleague a ride, answering small insults with more clever insults, even withholding friendship. All of those small gestures of revenge can make valid points; and they might provide a release for anger and justifiable outrage that might otherwise flare out of control.

But what interests me much more than revenge itself are those whose wrath or lust for revenge is ultimately transformed into something more ennobling. I am referring, of course, to those such as John Sage and his associates at Bridges to Life, people who emerge from a state of anger and rage to try to open prisoners' eyes and turn their attitudes around; or like Laura and David Blumenfeld, who insist on calling "revenge" what is really a successful attempt at transforming a formerly hostile soul.

"Revenge is a desire to not just punish the culprit, but to change his mind, to make him see, if only in his death throes, that he was wrong," observed Stephen Beckerman, an anthologist at Pennsylvania State University. As many of those who have gone through victim-offender mediation sessions attest, the desire to change minds can coexist with, indeed be motivated by, the drive for revenge. It can lend moral meaning to the fight for revenge. But it can also lead to an evolution beyond revenge, beyond the unthinking impulse to take an eye for an eye, a life for a life.

In the stories of Sage, Blumenfeld, Kurland, and Brown I see parables not merely, not even mostly, of revenge, but also of faith in the capacity of humans to change—faith, in other words, in the possibility of transformation. I see as well, living testaments to the ability of even the most aggrieved human beings to entertain and embrace the prospect of reconciliation, as they challenge the notion that grievous wrongs must inevitably be answered in kind.

4.

HARMONY OUT OF CHAOS

THE WORLD MAY BE MORE DANGEROUS THAN ever. And armed conflict shows no signs of going out of style. But despite continuing evidence of man's antagonistic inclinations—and due in part to the example of such powerful personalities as Archbishop Desmond Tutu and Nelson Mandela—reconciliation is in vogue. If perpetrator and victim could touch each other's soul, the world would be better for that touching, we are told. "People are beginning to think of forgiveness and reconciliation as spiritual values that have more significance than they had previously recognized," wrote Tutu, in his foreword to *Forgiveness and Reconciliation.*

But unlike forgiveness, which you can do on your own, which merely requires a certain softening of the heart, reconciliation requires a change in someone else, or at least a willingness on the parts of those who were estranged to form, if not a friendship, then at least something of an alliance; to agree, if nothing else, to be involved with one another—in a psychologically complex and intimate way.

Martin Macwan, founder of Navsarjan, a human rights organization in Ahmadabad, a city in India, intuitively understands the trade-offs reconciliation may require—especially when alliances are forged across a divide of religion and culture. Navsarjan provides legal and social services to the poor, primarily Dalits, formerly called Untouchables, in the state of Gujarat.

One day a woman from a higher-caste family showed up at Navsarjan. Some family members had been imprisoned and the woman was distraught. They needed bail; they needed a lawyer. And she had neither the money, the contacts, nor the knowledge to do anything on their behalf.

Given the scorn commonly heaped on Dalits by upper-caste people and the indignities, even murders and other atrocities, routinely suffered by the Dalits at the hands of the recognized elites, some of Macwan's colleagues thought he should toss the woman out. Instead, Macwan asked a fellow worker to give her a glass of water. The woman took the glass and stared at it, realizing that, since it came from an "Untouchable," she was forbidden by religious custom to drink. For several seconds she held the glass, trembling as he stared at her, his expression silently communicating a message: "You drink the water and I'll help you. But if you are not willing to risk your privileged social status, if you are unwilling to treat a Dalit as an equal, you walk out empty-handed." Finally, she took a sip.

From that day on, Macwan told me over lunch in Ahmadabad, he requires any higher-caste person who comes in looking for help to pass the water glass test: "If you want help from Navsarjan, you have to drink a glass of water from a Dalit family."

For Macwan, the story is about power and transformation: "You establish your leadership over others. You influence their actions and their hearts." It is also, however, about something considerably more subversive. It is about demanding respect that society withholds while building alliances that society forbids, about forcing people to question conventions that keep people who are considered different apart.

Reconciliation normally does not require an individual to question thousands of years of religious indoctrination. It mostly requires confronting personal history and weighing old injuries in light of current yearnings to reconnect. Yearnings of the sort felt by a woman I will call Cindy.

With her dark, straight hair, soulful gaze, and smooth olive complexion, Cindy looks like a Mediterranean beach beauty; but when she opens her mouth, the illusion vanishes. Her soft, melodic voice comes wrapped in an accent that is unmistakably urban, middle class, and East Coast.

Her father left when Cindy was nine. She and her younger sister went with the mother; the two sons from the father's previous marriage stayed with their dad. But the bond with the father endured. They spent weekends and summers together and often had dinner during the week.

The close relationship ended when Cindy was in her early thirties. Her father, who had always been mercurial, became enraged at being excluded from an important family meeting. He stayed away from the hospital when Cindy's son was born and subsequently made it clear that he wanted nothing to do with either her or her son. Six years later, when her mother was dying from cancer, Cindy thought his anger would abate. It didn't. Her father boycotted the funeral and didn't even call.

Several years passed, and her stepbrother alerted her that Dad was hospitalized and about to undergo a risky surgical procedure. Overcome with concern, Cindy called her father, and they talked as if they had never been estanged. Soon after the surgery, which went well, her father invited Cindy and her husband and son to dinner. The son, who was then ten, met his grandfather for the first time. Cindy noticed that her father was thinner and frailer, with arthritis in his hands—all those things brought home the reality of the passage of time and the importance of savoring it with loved ones while they were still alive.

The father apologized for being absent when Cindy's mother

died. And he promised to never disappear again. Cindy decided to take him at his word. "It's easier to forgive someone if you have your own needs for them," she concluded.

Reconciliation driven by love, memories, and the need to keep a family together is something we can all understand. But there are other forms of reconciliation much more challenging—that of a perpetrator and a victim, for instance, who have no love, no good memories to draw on, who are connected only by tragedy, and by the need to make sense of it and of the rest of their lives.

Walter Everett, pastor of the United Methodist Church of Hartford, Connecticut, was out of state in July 1987 when he learned that his twenty-four-year-old son, Scott, had been murdered. Everett rushed home and subsequently learned the circumstances and details of a killing that in a saner world would never have occurred.

Scott, the oldest of his two boys, after spending the night out with friends, had managed to lock himself out. His pounding on the outer door attracted the attention of a neighbor, Michael Carlucci, who happened to be somewhat paranoid and who was also high on cocaine. Carlucci came to the door with a gun in his hand. Although he should have recognized Scott, since in his capacity as manager of the apartment building, Carlucci had been collecting rent from him for the past two years, apparently he did not.

Words were exchanged and Carlucci ordered Scott to leave. Scott refused and Carlucci ended up shooting him. He was arrested shortly thereafter.

After returning to Connecticut, Everett went to the apartment building where Scott had been killed. He was not sure what he expected to find but thought he might discover something that would help convict the man who had killed his son. When he approached the detectives who had been assigned the case to discuss how his legwork might help, they brushed him off. "You don't need to do this. We've already made an arrest," one detective told him. Then the detective added—gratuitously in Everett's opinion—that he and his partner had dealt with several homicides that weekend. "We're burned out."

At that point, the anger and frustration welled up. Everett's son had been murdered for no reason, and the police didn't seem to be taking the case seriously. Over the next few months his gloom deepened. He went to a few meetings of a support group for families traumatized by murder but found the experience profoundly unsettling. Although he was grateful for the company and the consolation, he was surprised at the tremendous amount of anger in that room, anger that some people had carried for fifteen or twenty years. "I couldn't understand how anger could last that long." And he feared that if he didn't fight against it, his anger might harden as well; so he prayed for direction, but no path then appeared.

The following May the prosecutor called and told him that Carlucci had agreed to a plea bargain, not for murder but for second-degree manslaughter. His sentence would be ten years—only a fraction of which he would actually have to serve. Everett was astounded. "Do you think that's fair?" he asked. The prosecutor explained that the evidence was not strong enough to convict for murder. Recalling how cavalierly the detectives had treated him, how little input he had had at every juncture, Everett fumed as the realization sunk in that, when it came to the system, even though his son was the victim, he was little more than a bystander.

Nonetheless, he went to Carlucci's sentencing. And he was unexpectedly moved by Carlucci's apology. "I'm sorry I killed Scott. . . . I wish I could bring him back," said Carlucci, but he acknowledged that the words were futile. The twenty or so friends who had come to support Everett dismissed the apology as nothing more than a gesture calculated to impress the judge. But Everett was not so sure. The words brought a certain amount of comfort. In retrospect Everett came to see the plea bargain as something of a gift. For if Carlucci had been tried—and presumably had asserted and tried to prove his innocence—"I never would have heard him say, 'I'm sorry.' "

Carlucci's apology motivated Everett to write him a letter in which he tried to describe what Scott's loss had meant. He told Carlucci that he appreciated the apology and also told him that he felt as if God were prompting him to forgive. "I didn't feel forgiveness at the time," admitted Everett; but he knew he had to find some way to deal with the corrosive emotions coursing through his body. "I didn't have a good feeling about how I felt about myself. . . . I wanted to heal."

Everett later learned that when Carlucci received the letter, Carlucci assumed it would be an angry diatribe and refused to read it. Instead, he had a counselor open it for him. Only after the counselor had read it and urged him to do the same did Carlucci summon up the nerve to see what Everett had written. As Carlucci read, he wept; and too self-conscious to kneel on the floor, he kneeled on his bunk and prayed.

Several weeks later, Carlucci wrote back and thanked Everett for his letter. He apologized for taking so long to reply but explained that he had to get special permission to write to the father of the man he had killed.

At that point, Everett resolved to pay Carlucci a visit. He set a date in late November but got called away to two different funerals, which he took as a sign that the time was not quite right. He rescheduled for December 1988. The day he showed up at the maximum-security prison, they told him Carlucci had been moved to a medium-security prison down the road. Again, anger welled up. This man had killed his son and yet he was being coddled. Nonetheless, Everett continued down the road.

When he saw Carlucci, Everett tried to break the tension with an innocuous comment about Carlucci having gained weight. Carlucci replied that he had been living on drugs and alcohol before his incarceration and that prison food was an improvement. The ice broken, the two men talked easily, about God and their families. And when Everett got up to leave, it seemed right that they embraced instead of simply shaking hands.

That visit, said Everett, "forever changed both of our lives." He started going to the prison regularly to visit Carlucci. And he realized that the prisoner was changing, that the man who was becoming a friend was not the same man who had killed his son. When Carlucci went before the parole board two years after that first visit, Everett spoke on his behalf.

Carlucci ended up serving thirty-five months. After his release, he went to work for a trucking firm and soon became a supervisor. The two men stayed in touch; and sometime later, when Carlucci took a bride, Everett officiated. Carlucci's wife died a few years later, from an illness related to a prior drug addiction, and Everett helped him to bury her. The two remain in close touch.

"Victims don't need vengeance," Everett told me. "They need to hear somebody say 'I'm sorry' or find out what happened and why. . . . I don't know if I could have forgiven if I hadn't heard those words." Those words were sufficient motivation for Everett to begin the journey that ended with him embracing the man who had torn apart his life.

Obviously, reconciliation can be a long and demanding process. In Everett's case, it could only begin after Carlucci admitted and assumed personal responsibility for his crime. And even once that happened—and even though Everett felt God pushing him in that direction—reconciliation could only occur after the two had established a relationship of trust and after Everett had assured himself that Carlucci was a man transformed. After all that, healing still was a long time coming. How much longer must it take, how much more difficult could it be, when it is a whole nation that must reconcile?

In proposing a truth commission to investigate race relations in the United States, Archbishop Desmond Tutu waxed typically poetical. "Hear the anguish in each other's hearts. And yes, the wound will be opened, but the wound will be cleansed and balm poured over the wound; and it will heal and will not fester," he told a hushed, multiracial gathering in Birmingham, Alabama, in April 2002.

Isabel Amaral-Guterres, who was trained as a nurse, used almost identical language on the website of East Timor's truth and reconciliation commission, of which she was a member: "In East Timor we need to remember for a little while, open up the wounds, so that they can be healed and we can move on, carrying the scars but not the infection."

But what exactly does reconciliation and healing mean in such a context? And how well do we understand how to bring such things about? Is it realistic to expect entire nations to go through a process as emotionally demanding and as dependent on faith—in God, in one's fellow man—as Everett and Carlucci went through? On what basis are they to be reconciled? And how broad can that reconciliation be?

In the case of Everett and Carlucci, it was very clear who was the victim and who was the victimizer. Most nations cannot so easily be divided along such lines. How much can Tutu's stirring message about healing and reconciliation apply to an undifferentiated mass of people who are connected by citizenship but disconnected by experiences and often by culture as well? While nations certainly consist of people, nations are not human beings. They do not hurt in quite the same way. They do not love the same way. Nor do they heal or forgive in the same fashion.

Cindy and her dad were ultimately brought together because of deep reservoirs of love and need; they were bound to each other in a way that only a family or something approximating a family can be bound. Whatever relationship the Afrikaners may have to the Zulus or Xhosas of South Africa, or the Dalits may have to the Vaisyas or Brahmans of India, it is not the same as that connecting a daughter to a father—or a brother to a sister.

So I'm inclined to view the idea of a nation healing by passing through some sort of collective catharsis with a certain amount of skepticism. I see precious little evidence that nations heal in quite that manner—if they heal collectively at all. Impressive as South Africa's TRC experiment was—and it was truly inspirational in a great many respects—it did not turn South Africa into one big family. Nor given the TRC's limitations, and South Africa's history, could it have hoped to bring everybody together—notwithstanding all the high-flown rhetoric around the commission's formation and the often compelling drama of its hearings.

In his foreword to Eugene de Kock's memoir, *A long night's DAMAGE*, South African journalist Jeremy Gordin wrote of a young black man who came to de Cock's TRC hearing. "There he is, there is the fucking bastard I want to see!" exclaimed the man when de Kock took the stand. Reflecting on the outburst, Gordin was moved to observe: "Understandably, those hurt by apartheid want palpable redress. And, although the proceedings of the Truth Commission have given this to them to some extent, the proceedings have perhaps been too drawn out, too quasi-legalistic and too tempered by the Christian goodwill of its chairman, Archbishop Desmond Tutu, to satisfy that most elemental urge: revenge. More effective might have been a series of trials— prosecuted according to the best that 20th-century law has to offer, not in terms of 'reconciliation.'"

One of the things that made reconciliation possible for Everett and Carlucci is that Carlucci accepted personal responsibility and faced some—albeit small—punishment for the awful thing he had done. In South Africa, the same amnesty provision that lured perpetrators to the witness box—and it was, indeed, the price for a peaceful transition—prevented anyone from truly accepting personal responsibility. For that provision required that petitioners argue, in order to qualify for amnesty, that their actions were compelled, fomented, or otherwise caused by their government or political organization. So they could apologize, but it was an incomplete, conditional, very likely insincere apology:

I'm very, very sorry for what I did and for the great suffering I caused;
but the state made me do it. I was only trying to be a good citizen.

Nor did the process require, as did Martin Macwan of non-Dalits, that the representatives of the perpetrator group surrender their status, that they humble themselves before the object of their previous disdain. And because there was no leveling process, no equalizing of status, the reconciliation that occurred, even between individuals, was suspiciously superficial; for it came at no—or relatively little—cost to those who had done so much wrong.

More to the point, however, is the fact that reconciliation between a few individuals does not necessarily lead to reconciliation between all members of the group they supposedly represent. It is one thing to hurt collectively. For when it comes to suffering, members of targeted groups often have no choice. It's a lot harder to heal collectively. In South Africa, the black majority was oppressed as a group, so they naturally shared a sense of collective pain. But they were not repaired as a group; nor were they reconciled as a group; and they were certainly not integrated into mainstream society and commerce as a group.

From the beginning, the family of Steve Biko, the South African black-consciousness leader who died in police custody in 1977, was skeptical of the TRC approach. His killers, family members thought, did not deserve amnesty but ought to be prosecuted. So they went to court in a failed attempt to block the TRC from considering amnesty applications from five former cops who admitted being with Biko when he died.

In a conversation in 2002, Nkosinathi Biko, Steve Biko's younger brother and chair of the foundation named in his honor, explained some of his frustrations with the process. "You go in there and hope that they tell the truth, and if they didn't tell the truth that was it. . . . You've got no recourse. . . . The five that applied for amnesty in the Steve Biko case were certainly not deserving. Prior to them making these presentations in public, we had read some of their summations. All of them applied for amnesty . . . but none of them agreed they had interacted with him in a manner that brought about his death."

They did admit beating him and lying about when he died; but beatings, they explained, were permitted in the South Africa of the time. And they insisted Biko's death was caused not by the beating but when he accidentally bumped his head. The TRC rejected their arguments and their amnesty applications; but they were not prosecuted.

"It would have been very interesting," said Nkosinathi Biko, "to have been confronted with a genuine apology from the killers of Steve Biko—something, of course, we never got. . . . I'm sure that would have appealed to me at some human level."

Like many black South Africans, Biko also noted that a relatively small number of whites attended the hearings. If you were neither a designated victim nor a perpetrator, you really didn't have to participate. And many people, especially white South Africans, chose to tune it out—at least to the extent they could, given the massive coverage that some of the hearings received. The proceedings, concluded Biko, were essentially "a case of black people listening to their own story."

"In many societies there is a role for some mythology," added Biko. "The problem is the expectations that we have of the mythology. And I think the expectations we had of the mythology here were just way, way beyond what the mythology could deliver. . . . I think also the international community invested so much of its own hope in this commission that there was a certain denial even internationally about the fact that it may not have worked out the way that it was expected."

Even some of the TRC's biggest fans believe it was much better at unearthing truth than at fostering reconciliation. And that truth, revealing and shocking in many instances as it was, was necessarily limited—particularly from the perspective of many of the "victims" who were looking for some very precise answers to some extremely difficult questions: *How was he killed? How much did he suffer? Who informed on him? Where are his remains? Where are his killers? Why did it have to happen?*

Many of the answers, not surprisingly, were not forthcoming. "Most victims clearly wanted some kind of truth from the TRC," said Hugo van der Merwe, projects manager in the Transition and Reconciliation Unit of the Centre for the Study of Violence and Reconciliation, "and not just the truth of their own stories being told and acknowledged as true; they wanted more information, more facts about who the killers were. . . . Who ordered the torture, etcetera. . . . And I would say that ninety-five percent of the people didn't get that kind of detail."

Even for designated victims—those who gave testimony and, in many cases, saw their perpetrators attempting to answer for their crimes—there was not one TRC experience but several. "Some people have gotten substantial information; some of them have gotten a sense of recognition, of healing; and some of them have gotten nothing," said van der Merwe. Their experiences reflected not only the differences in how their cases were handled, but also differences in their expectations. Some people were looking for details on exactly what their son or husband had contributed to the cause. Some were looking for recognition that family members did not betray friends when they were tortured. And some were seeking vindication for loved ones they felt had been unfairly portrayed.

There was also, van der Merwe believes, a certain "inequality amongst different victims." Those who had the high-profile cases, the ones certain to attract media interest, were, of course, the focus of a great deal of attention. "The result was a certain marginalization of people who didn't feel their cases were seen as important as others by the TRC."

None of this means the South Africa's TRC was a failure. Indeed, considered alongside most similar commissions—and, indeed, alongside political bodies generally—it was a raging success. But there are some things beyond the power of commissions. And national reconciliation is likely among them.

In Peru, those associated with that country's identically named Truth and Reconciliation Commission *(Comisión de la Verdad y Reconciliación)* acknowledged that reality up front. When I asked TRC commissioner and sociologist Sofía Macher Batanero what she believed people expected from her commission, she was strikingly humble. People's first expectation was justice, that people would be punished for the widespread abuses that had been committed. Secondly, they expected some form of reparations for their loss or suffering. And much further down on the list, she said, was some hope of reconciliation. But even justice and reparations, she pointed out, were not in the commission's power to deliver. They could only recommend.

The atrocities committed by the militia and the guerrilla groups—the Shining Path (which apparently accounted for the majority of the deaths) and the Tupac Amaru Revolutionary Movement—were committed primarily against poor people and disproportionately against nonwhites. Particularly hard hit were members of the country's indigenous groups who spoke Quechua or other native tongues. They accounted for perhaps three-fourths of all those murdered. And many privileged Peruvians were quite willing to close their eyes to the effects of that political violence on the most vulnerable members of society. "For many Peruvians, what happened in the Sierra or in the jungle is somebody else's problem," observed Viviana Valz Gen Rivera, of the TRC's mental health team.

Valz Gen saw the TRC's efforts as part of a larger process of helping the country confront not only some horrible truths about the militia and the guerrillas but also its own ambivalence. There are things that happened that people really don't want to hear about "because it's very painful," she said. Part of the reason many people didn't have to face those things earlier is that a premium was placed on silence: people "learned silence as a way of saving their lives."

Francisco Soberon, director of the National Coordinating Board of Human Rights Organizations, a nongovernmental coalition, saw the commission's role, in part, as ending that culture of silence, of helping to open people's eyes and ears. "It's an opportunity to hear . . . the voices of the victims, their truth. Most of the victims were indigenous peasant people from the highlands. . . . For the first time, people are realizing the atrocities. . . . This is an important process for all Peruvians to realize what happened—the first experience in Latin America where there are public hearings."

An estimated 69,280 of Peru's citizens were killed by political violence between May 1980 and November 2000. That period constituted the "most intense, most extensive and most prolonged" episode of violence in the country's history, noted the commission in its final report presented to President Alejandro Toledo at the end of August 2003. That the commission was not only acknowledging such massive wrongdoing but was also charged with trying to understand how and why it happened symbolized a significant change in the know-nothing culture—one about which TRC commissioners were understandably elated.

"In a country like Peru, the commission offers a singular opportunity for Peruvian society to choose its best destiny," observed Salomón Lerner Febres, a philosopher and the commission president. The commission's role, as he saw it, was not merely to be the custodian of "historical memory" but also to move the country in a more democratic direction. But as for forgiveness and reconciliation? Forgiveness, he pointed out, was not a thing that could be mandated.

Peru, of course, has no figure comparable to Mandela or Tutu, no living paragons of forgiveness and compassion preaching the gospel of harmony and togetherness. It also has no analogue to apartheid, whose very existence, in dividing the country into such discrete groups, provided an irresistible backdrop for the pageant of reconciliation.

In Peru, unlike in South Africa, amnesty was not part of the commission's mandate. Former president Alberto Fujimori had pardoned the military and the police in 1995. Although that pardon was later revoked by the Inter-American Court of Human Rights, the TRC had no desire and no power to revisit the question. Nor did Peru's TRC provide much of a stage for perpetrators—although people accused of illegal acts did have the right to reply. So there was no real opportunity for the emotional drama of perpetrator and victim confronting each other and, perhaps, collapsing into each other's arms. What was on display was the suffering of victims. And the wounds, years after their infliction, were painfully raw—as I discovered when I accompanied some of the commission staff to a regional hearing.

The night we arrived in Tarapoto, a small town in the jungle region *(la selva)*, a rally for the commission was held in the center of town. Townspeople assembled around a makeshift stage where yellow candles illuminated large mounted photographs of loved ones who had disappeared. Many of those in attendance held signs: PEACE *[Paz]* IS NOT ONLY THREE LETTERS BUT A DREAM THAT CAN BE A REALITY read one. THOUSANDS HAVE SUFFERED read another. HOW WAS THIS POSSIBLE? asked a third.

There was prayer and singing and young performers dancing; and there was much oratory and talk of truth, and faith, and the future. The hearings were held the next morning at a Catholic church in the town center. On either side of the stage where witnesses appeared were nine large pictures portraying people who were either dead or had disappeared (the *desaparecidos).* There was also a sign reading, PERUVIANS HAVE THE RIGHT TO THE TRUTH.

As people testified—many crying as they talked—a picture emerged of an area that had been trapped in a continuing nightmare, terrorized by soldiers or guerrillas who might strike anyone at any time, for no particular reason. The army, the police, the Shining Path, the Tupac Amaru Revolutionary Movement—or MRTA: *Movimiento Revolucionario Tupac Amaru*—were equally anarchistic, killing on a whim. People told of being arrested without cause and accused of being terrorists and drug dealers. One woman testified that after her release, she was so terrified that she still could not look a soldier or policeman in the eye. And she, in a relative sense, was among the lucky ones.

There was testimony from the family of a journalist who wrote a story about six church members who were assassinated by the police. Following the story's publication, the cops came to his mother's house and roughed up his mother and brother. The journalist went to the station house to demand an explanation and was never seen again.

Two sisters told of MRTA commandos bursting into their home and kidnapping their father. Later, they found their dad's body riddled with bullets—they had pierced his heart, mouth, and elsewhere—and his arms were tied together.

During a break, I spoke to several witnesses, including two cops, who had spent thirty-six months in jail for investigating people who had powerful friends. They had been out of prison for several years; but they still seemed somewhat in a state of shock, wondering how such a thing could have happened to them, wondering how they could begin to recover their lives.

That afternoon I heard the most grisly story of the day. Over a lunch of spicy, shredded pork, a tiny, soft-spoken woman told of soldiers coming on a Sunday morning and pulling her and her husband out of bed. They taped her mouth, tied her hands, and beat her until her breasts and arms were bruised. Ignoring her husband's pleas to leave his wife alone, the soldiers tossed the couple into a truck. In all, the invaders took over thirty people to the bank of a river, lined them up, and shot each in the back of the head. The woman fell to the ground, her mouth full of blood; but somehow she survived; her face was permanently scared and her front teeth shattered as a result of that shooting. The soldiers completed their work by tossing all the bodies, including hers, into the water. She managed to crawl out of the water and eventually to find help and, to the extent possible, recover; but she still feared the people who had wreaked so much havoc might someday return to finish the job. She was talking to the commission staff, behind a veil of anonymity, in the hope they might be able to guarantee her safety.

The next day, I visited Lamas, a village located a short distance from Tarapoto. With roosters crowing in the background, residents gathered in a semicircle and told of a day during the 1990s when the militia arrived. "They said they were looking for members of the Shining Path, but no one belonged to the Shining Path," said a thin, elderly man. Nonetheless, a helicopter appeared, people were blindfolded, and in three separate trips, the helicopter carted off dozens of villagers.

What were they hoping to accomplish by telling the commission their story?

"We hope to receive justice," answered a villager.

"What kind of justice?" I asked.

"To know what is the truth—what happened to the people."

Later in Lima, I asked Eduardo González Cueva, who worked in the public hearings unit, why forgiveness and reconciliation were emphasized so much less in Peru than in South Africa.

In a largely Christian country like Peru, he replied, it would have been easy to stress forgiveness, to try to force people to reconcile. But forgiveness, he added, was a gift—one that should be given freely. Also, there was the fear factor. In order to reconcile with your tormenter you must be confident that the person who harmed you is not going to do it again. And though the various sides in Peru had put down arms, they had not really renounced what they had done. But perhaps most importantly, he added, reconciliation had to be rooted in fundamental change. "Reconciliation means to build a different society, a society that is more fair, more decent, not racist, and not *machista*. And that is the work of generations."

The commission's final report made essentially the same point. It endorsed an ambitious plan of restitution and reparations, but it also called for much more. It recommended a program of education and health care for those poor citizens most affected by the violence. And it suggested myriad ways of acknowledging their suffering: a card from the president to each victim apologizing for the tragedy; a national day of tribute to those who had been victimized; suitable memorials in parks and other public places. It also urged that more perpetrators be brought to justice. And it called for reconciliation rooted in a dramatic change in the attitudes of Peruvian society. It urged Peruvians to reject the assumption that the murder of poor, indigenous peasants was somehow all right.

In his letter transmitting the final report to President Toledo, chairman Salomón Lerner Febres put forth his vision of the new Peru. He evoked the dream that, as he saw it, was present at the nation's birth, a dream of "a country of human beings equal in dignity where the death of each citizen counts as a personal tragedy and in which each lost life—whether the result of an atrocity, a crime, or an abuse—puts in motion the wheels of justice to compensate for the loss and to punish those responsible."

If societal reconciliation is truly about building a new and different society then East Timor has a huge advantage. The former Portuguese colony was occupied from 1975 through much of 1999 by Indonesia. In May 2002 it came into the world a new—and newly independent—nation, under the watchful eye of the United Nations. It was a country literally created out of chaos. During the years of an often-violent Indonesian occupation and freedom struggle, as many as 200,000 East Timorese out of a total population of less than 800,000 ended up dead. Following the vote for independence in August 1999, pro-Indonesia militias went on a final rampage. Hundreds were killed, tens of thousands of homes were destroyed, and virtually the entire population, terrified, took to the hills. By the time independence arrived, there was a great deal to reconcile and a hunger for harmony. And as has become the rage with emerging democracies, East Timor appointed a truth commission—or, as the East Timorese called it, a Commission for Reception, Truth and Reconciliation.

The key question confronting commissioners as well as the rest of East Timor's leadership was, "How do you reconcile a country that was born out of a conflict so violent that perhaps a fourth of its population died as a result—a conflict that set villager against villager and caused massive numbers to flee?" As Jake Moreland, of the office of the UN High Commissioner for Refugees, observed, "Reconciliation was needed here from day one."

When we met in late 2002, Moreland was pondering the plight of thousands of Timorese who had fled to West Timor, where many of them cowered in fear "of what the communities will do to them," as Moreland put it, if they decided to return. Many of them—apparently most—eventually did return; but to get some sense of why they were so fearful, one need only reflect for a moment on what they and their confederates had done.

In a district of East Timor called Liquica, a small white stone monument in Liquica Church pays tribute to lives lost to unbridled violence. On the monument was an empty space, presumably for a photograph, along with a metal Jesus on the cross. In the church are small living quarters roughly the size of a small living room. In April 1999 that church, that room, was the site of a massacre.

The period was one of heavy intermittent violence—from which villagers sought refuge in the church. In April that violence crescendoed into a two-day siege. During the rampage, members of the local militia and Indonesian troops fired guns into the air and destroyed numerous houses. And they eventually turned their attention to the terrified villagers huddled together in the church.

They attacked the church with tear gas, and as the townspeople tried to escape, the soldiers fell upon them with rifles, machetes, knives, automatic firearms, and other weapons. They relentlessly pursued those who tried to flee. By the time the melee was over, upward of a hundred villagers were dead or seriously injured. As part of the cover-up that followed the unprovoked assault, soldiers dumped bodies, by the truckload, into a lake.

When I talked to Father Albino Marques, the current priest,

about the difficulty of welcoming back wrongdoers who had fled, he replied, "When they come back, we must receive them. We must make meetings, talk to them. We must make a dialogue."

Making a dialogue is a big thing in East Timor, and it's part of the reconciliation process actively promoted by the Catholic church in this heavily Catholic country. Natalia do Menino Jesus Ferreiro, a nun in the nearby subdistrict of Maubara, acknowledged that it was sometimes difficult making villagers understand that they should forgive. "People say it's difficult to forgive." By the same token, she said, many of those who fled did not believe they would be forgiven. She had met several on a visit to a refugee camp who worried they would be killed if they dared to return.

Father Jovito Araujo, vice chairman of the reconciliation commission, told me about a meeting that he had attended between villagers and a wrongdoer who had decided to return. The man, who brought all his belongings to the community meeting, admitted burning the possessions of others. Pointing to his own belongings, he said, "If you want to burn it, do it. If you want to do something to me, do it." Instead of attacking him, the people cried and hugged him. "Now he is protected," said Araujo. If a person returned in the proper way, with humility, respect, and willingness to try to set things right, "We will forgive everything," he added.

I asked him about the commission's name. Why *Reception, Truth and Reconciliation?* The word *reception* was translated from the Portuguese *alcolhimento*—which means "welcome" or "refuge." But as used by the commission, explained Araujo, there was a strong spiritual component to the concept, one reflected in Luke 15, the parable of the prodigal son.

And the son said unto him, Father, I have sinned against heaven, and in thy sight, and am no more worthy to be called thy son.

But the father said to his servants, Bring forth the best robe, and put it on him; and put a ring on his hand, and shoes on his feet:

And bring hither the fatted calf, and kill it; and let us eat, and be merry:

For this my son was dead, and is alive again; he was lost, and is found. And they began to be merry.

It was important, he said, that those who fought for independence welcome back those who fought with the militia. "Who will be the father who will bring together these conflicting brothers?" he asked rhetorically. "Maybe the commission will be the father. . . . Our people are a religious people; they understand it."

In a small village where people were working at a CARE-funded water sanitation project, I went looking for that understanding. Thanks to CARE, they would no longer have to trek more than six hundred meters for water. They were grateful for CARE's efforts. And they spoke proudly of the freedom they had, now that East Timor was a democracy. But they were unsure how warm the welcome would be for those Timorese—the takers of lives, the destroyers of homes—who might decide to return.

"If we can talk together . . . we will not create the violence," one man told me. But on reflection, he added, "The government must have justice for them. . . . The government doesn't need to take their home. Children and wife can stay in their home; but get them to a tribunal."

The response was much the same from a *suco* chief, or local leader, in another village I visited that day. Luis Faria Araujo, a lean handsome man with dark hair, a mustache, and wrinkled face, looked much older than his forty years. He was confident, said Arujo, that his people would happily "receive" those coming back if they had not committed really serious crimes. If they had destroyed someone's property, maybe they would plant a garden for the community as a form of penance and compensation. But if their crimes were serious, he said, they would have to go to prison.

I raised the issue of *reception* with East Timor's president, Xanana

Gusmao, a vigorous charismatic former leader of the fight for liberation whose compassion and faith in reconciliation evoke com-
parisons to Nelson Mandela. Gusmao described a visit he had
made to a village, during which the inhabitants had talked of the
need to punish or arrest those who had committed abuses during
the era of violence in East Timor. He had pointed out that East
Timor is a very poor country, with very few resources. Should
those resources go primarily for prisons, he asked, or schools,
medical care, education, things that could change the quality of
their lives? "If I ask to kill people who did this, will that change
my life?" he asked.

In the end, he said, the people got his point. "Before they were
asking me to put all criminals in jail. . . . Now they ask me to con-
vey their need to UNTAT"—the United Nations Transitional
Authority on East Timor, the body responsible for getting East
Timor on its feet.

"We need to give to our children a new environment," said
Gusmao. There was no point in carrying grudges into the next
generation. There was a need to move beyond revenge. And he
had faith his people "will see the better way to forget the past is to
improve their lives." Just as he had faith that local justice—
arrived at by sitting in a village and engaging in dialogue, perhaps
after everyone had been ritually sprinkled with chicken blood—
would yield much better results than trying to prosecute everyone
who had committed a crime. That process, one rooted in indigenous principles of reconciliation, "buys people a safe place back in
their community and nothing else can do that."

There was not only idealism to what Gusmao had to say but also
a large dose of pragmatism. East Timor clearly lacked the capacity
to launch a major prosecutorial effort. There were not enough
lawyers, not enough judges, not enough police, not enough investigators, and merely the suggestion—as opposed to the reality—of a
judicial system. Inevitably, many offenders, most offenders, were
fated to go free. "Formal justice is impossible," said Gusmao. "It's

something else, or nothing." The energy, he said, must go into building, not vengeance.

But there were some cases, those considered particularly serious, that East Timor felt it had an obligation to prosecute. Siri Frigaard, a prosecutor from Norway, was one of those brought in by the United Nations to help East Timor build a justice system. She was also drafting indictments for the prosecution of serious crimes—including the Liquica massacre. Like Gusmao, she recognized the impossibility of prosecuting everyone and was therefore focusing only on crimes of the most serious nature.

What exactly was a serious crime? And which, among them, were likely to be prosecuted?

"One person burns one house, that is probably less serious," said Frigaard. "One other has burned ten houses. That is a serious crime; but we can't do anything with it." Now the wrongdoer who killed a person and stole a goat—that would rise to the level of something meriting prosecution, although a judgment would have to be made about whether to devote the resources to prosecute it. Then there were priority cases, clear and outrageous crimes against humanity, crimes such as the massacres at the Liquica Church, the Suai Church, and elsewhere. They would prosecute such cases to the full extent of their ability and the law; but Frigaard was more than a little bit worried about having to make such Solomonic and sometimes arbitrary distinctions.

She also worried about those crimes—and criminals—who would fall through the cracks, those considered not serious enough for her serious crimes unit but too serious to be left to a village reception process or to the truth and reconciliation commission.

Commission chairman Aniceto Guterres Lopes accepted the impossibility of making coherent legal sense of the situation in East Timor, or of prosecuting any more than a fraction of those who had committed various crimes. But he also thought the lust for vengeance in East Timor was not terribly strong because

Timorese realized that even the perpetrators were not totally to blame.

"Every Timorese realizes that we killed one another," he said. "They also realize the killing of each other was caused by forces outside—external factors. We don't need to hate each other anymore."

I was intrigued by Guterres Lopes's argument for diminished responsibility for the perpetrators. For he was essentially saying that even though the perpetrators were responsible, they were not totally responsible, because they had been co-opted—as had the entire country—by a powerful, occupying power, which effectively shifted much of the fault for their atrocities to Indonesia (a country that, not surprisingly, had little interest in vigorously prosecuting those perpetrators who still resided there). By contrast, in South Africa, there has been no occupying power; so while perpetrators argued that they were merely following orders, those orders did not arise from some hostile, foreign entity but from higher-ups right at home. So if there was any residual blame to place, it had to be placed on fellow South Africans. From the point of view of a nation trying to reconcile by squarely placing blame—if not exactly responsibility—for the wrongs of the past, it seemed to me that East Timor, from a psychological point of view at least, had the advantage.

And that was not the only advantage East Timor had. In South Africa, the TRC became the would-be reconciler of people at very different strata—indeed at opposite ends—of society. There was a privileged class and a disadvantaged class, with membership allocated almost exclusively along racial lines; and the TRC was expected to bridge the divide. Inevitably, many questioned whether that was possible or made sense. To repeat the words of Thandi Shezi: "If I say, 'I reconciled with my perpetrator and my perpetrator is now a station commander and is earning fifty thousand rands a month and I'm living in a shack,' can you call that reconciliation?" In East Timor, the class and color divisions were hardly so stark. Reconciliation was not being sought between the rich and the poor, between blacks and whites, but between people who were in essentially identical circumstances but happened to pick different political sides. Also, East Timor was such a small country it was plausible to think of reconciliation as something that happened person to person, perpetrator to village, as opposed to by proxy and via TV.

Yet even for a country like East Timor, it seemed to me that societal reconciliation—social harmony—if it had any meaning at all, was not just about the relationship between perpetrators and former victims but, as Gusmao himself argued, about the quality of people's daily lives—and of how those people, far from the hot lights of a hearing room, related to each other on a daily basis.

While the head of East Timor's most important human rights organization nearly two years prior to his appointment to the reconciliation commission, Guterres Lopes wrote an essay of advice to his fellow Timorese—who were then readying themselves for the final push toward independence: "After inhaling the air of freedom from the Indonesian occupation, we must now begin building the new East Timorese nation-state. To be successful, this new nation-state must result in a new society that is free from a past full of oppression, human rights violations, and injustice. It must be a society that inspires the entire population to respect the law, human rights, democracy, and social justice. . . . In this matter, reconciliation is more than a political effort shaped by apologies, handshakes, and embraces."

Reconciliation is such a beautiful concept, but it is exceedingly hard to pin down—even in tiny East Timor. And in the huge country that is the United States it is infinitely harder. So I wondered about Tutu's suggestion that Americans needed a truth and reconciliation commission to set things right. What could such a body conceivably achieve?

That question took me to Greensboro, North Carolina, where in 2003 a group of folks had assembled to follow Tutu's advice.

They were organizing a Truth and Community Reconciliation Project, modeled after South Africa's TRC. Their commission, unlike the TRC, was not to look at human rights violations across the board but at one specific, shameful incident.

That incident, known as the Greensboro massacre, took place on November 3, 1979. The deadly explosion had been building for a long time—and was preceded by a series of events that pitted blacks against whites, industrialists against workers, and self-declared Communists against the Ku Klux Klan. A multiracial coalition of activists—many of whom belonged to the Workers Viewpoint Organization, which later became the Communist Workers Party—was trying to unionize workers in the area's textile mills. The Klan, with the apparent implicit support of the area's industrial elite, mobilized against those efforts and spread the word that unionizing could lead to blacks bossing white folks around.

Several months prior to the fatal showdown, the Klan, as part of an organizing drive, had sponsored a showing of *Birth of a Nation*. D.W. Griffith's brilliant, deeply racist, yet wildly popular film—it was the highest grossing film ever, when released in 1915—is a mythic take on a particular slice of southern history. It purports to show how sex-starved black imbeciles nearly destroyed the South; in Griffith's version of reality, the heroic KKK saved the day. The WVO disrupted the film showing and confronted the Klan. Subsequently the WVO planned a "Death to the Klan" rally in Greensboro for November.

The day of the march, heavily armed self-declared Klansmen and Nazis showed up at the scene. The police mysteriously disappeared; and Klansmen and Nazis opened fire on the crowd. They killed five and wounded several others before climbing into their vehicles and racing off. Although the event was captured on videotape, no one was ever convicted of murder. The state's trial exonerated the killers in 1980, and a federal trial did the same in 1984. The following year, the marchers won their sole legal vic-

tory. A civil court found several of the assailants and two policemen liable for the death of one of the protestors.

For years, some people in Greensboro have wrestled with the
meaning of that series of events. How could a city considered so
enlightened allow murderers caught on tape to go free? Why had
the police vanished at the very moment when they were most
needed? What was the relationship between the Klan and the
industrial elite, for whom the Klansmen so eagerly went to war?
And what did it all say about the so-called decent folks of
Greensboro that the murderers were never held responsible for
their acts? Had the killers known all along they would find sanctuary among the good, decent folk of Greensboro? Had they
made a deal with the cops?

To Zeb "Z" Holler, a Greensboro minister and cochair of the
reconciliation project, the fact that such a massacre could happen
and the killers go free meant that something was very wrong with
Greensboro, something unacknowledged and obscured by "a
cloud of forgetfulness, denial." "The truth has never been told,
never been broadly known in the community," said Holler. "We
learn from our experiences, and when experience is covered over
or misrepresented, you learn the wrong stuff."

Ken Massey, another minister involved with the effort, agreed
that the tragedy was not just an incident from the past but something that continued to haunt present-day Greensboro. He saw a
truth commission providing "a portal, a way to talk about something that's still wrong about our community, something that's
still broken." For Carolyn Coleman, a county commissioner, the
project was largely about healing: "I believe until the healing
takes place individually, the city can never reach its zenith. . . . It
will prepare us to move forward."

Nelson Johnson, one of the leaders of the abortive 1979 rally
and a member of the truth commission organizing group, saw the
effort as something that would raise the consciousness of the
entire community. It would provide not only the truth of the

events that had taken place but a larger truth that would allow the people of Greensboro to understand how the South of that day truly operated, and help them to understand the real role of the Klan in southern society. Unless Greensboro faced those truths, the city would "remain handcuffed to a whole interlocking network of false assumptions. . . . People don't have a way of cleansing distorted, collective memory." The commission, he believed, could "create a set of conditions" that would allow that cleansing to take place.

Alex Boraine, who served with Tutu on South Africa's TRC, dispatched a staff member from his Institute for Transitional Justice to advise the Greensboro group's efforts. He also convinced Tutu to make time to address the organizers. For Boraine, whose life is devoted to promoting and advising "transitional justice" efforts, helping the good people of Greensboro go about the business of healing was a natural thing to do. But he also had a larger vision. In Greensboro—population: 223,000—he saw "kind of a microcosm of what really ails the country . . . at least in terms of race and history." And he felt it possible the city's truth commission "could just be a symbol other communities would learn from." And even if it did not bring about a broad self-awareness in society, if it just manages to alleviate the suffering of survivors, to allow them to finally tell their story, "I'll think it was worthwhile."

The former mayor and reconciliation project cochair Carolyn Allen acknowledged that the initiative was not popular with everyone. "There are people who feel very strongly this is a backward-looking effort." But she thought otherwise. "You can't move forward until you get some of the recurring bumps out of your history." Why had she not tried to set things straight a few years earlier when she was mayor? "I did not find enough willingness within the structure or the city or on the part of the council to take on a major city-sponsored investigation."

It was not at all clear to me that the powers of Greenboro had become any more willing to probe the events of 1979 since Allen had left office in December 1999. When I asked the current mayor, Keith Holliday, his opinion of the commission, he pronounced it an absurd idea that had come along at a particularly bad time.

"Right now we are very sensitive to the image we are portraying to the rest of the country," he said, since the city was trying to bolster its weakened economy. Certainly, the 1979 incident was horrible and the failure to convict incomprehensible. "After hearing what I heard and viewing the videotape, I was shocked when there were no guilty verdicts. I would have found *somebody* guilty." Nonetheless, "we want to put it behind us." Why conjure up a "twenty-three-year-old painful memory" in the service of a project that is unlikely to lead to anything productive?

Coming after all the trials, and with all the evidence that had already been heard, Holliday doubted a commission with no official standing could uncover any important new truths. "There is value in examining this horrible incident," he said, but perhaps in a university setting where experts might tease out some history lessons. But the commission was an inherently politicized animal that was likely to do more harm than good to the community.

He also rejected the notion that a new inquiry could heal. For one thing, most of the community seemed to have healed just fine: "Nobody talks about it except as an incident in history. . . . I don't hear a hue and cry anywhere except in those closely associated with the surviving family members and friends. . . . Basically, it is not a burning issue. . . . Greensboro has moved on." And for those who haven't moved on, whose wounds were still open, he wondered whether any process would suffice. If you lost a child, killed by a drunk driver perhaps, "do you ever completely heal?" he asked. "Would you not always have a hole in your heart?"

But isn't the testifying, and the attendant acknowledgment of the wrong that was done, healing in and of itself—if not completely, at least enough to make the enterprise worthwhile? In reflecting on South Africa's TRC victims, Hugo van der Merwe made a telling point: "For a lot of victims, this was the first time that they told what their story was. They had kept it closed inside them. . . . Now whether that's good or bad depends on what happens after you open up . . . whether you do get more support. Do you get psychological counseling? Do you get acknowledgment from your community?" Or, as happened with Thandi Shezi, do you end up feeling you have been victimized again?

Can Greensboro, as a city, be healed by a TRC's labors? Can America's wounds be reopened and cleansed and soothed with a healing balm? I suspect that Holliday's view is reasonably on target. It's extremely difficult to convince groups of people who see no need for collective healing to get deeply involved in a process that supposedly will heal them—or heal their community. It's even more difficult when that process requires them to acknowledge so-called truths that their very self-image requires that they reject or deny.

Who, among the leading lights of Greensboro, present or past, is ready to accept the notion that he, or his dad or granddad, provided support and polite cover for the vile butchery of the Ku Klux Klan? Or that the positions they so proudly enjoy were won through stealing the labor of others who were brutally mistreated and had no way to defend themselves? Or that, at the very time city leaders were promoting their supposedly enlightened views, they were not disinclined to using violence to exclude—or control—those who didn't fit their mold? Why even bring up such cockeyed notions that are not only untrue, they would say, but irrelevant?

And if there is no appetite for acknowledging such things, there is clearly even less for accepting responsibility for them. Decent people—and who but sociopaths think of themselves in any other way?—were, of course, only doing the decent thing. If they tolerated a bit of evil, it was not because they supported it but because they were powerless against it. They too in a sense were victims.

And, if, in the end, there is no collective acknowledgment—at least that is meaningful to those who feel wronged—how does the healing take place? This dynamic, of course, does not apply just to Greensboro. There is a natural tendency among those who have the most privilege, and presumably also wield the most influence, to reject being implicated in anything impure or unfair—even if, *especially if,* they reap the benefits of that unfairness.

So in Peru, the moneyed class in the suburbs of Lima professed no knowledge of the outrages being committed supposedly on their behalf at the time that they occurred. Even now there is a certain ambivalence about that knowledge. As Viviana Valz Gen Rivera put it, "The country both wants and does not want to know." It is impossible today, one bemused black South African observed, to find any white South African who ever believed in apartheid. Apartheid, it seems, just happened. Nobody—nobody alive at any rate—was responsible for keeping it going. And certainly nobody supported it. Not really. It just sort of kept going on its own, almost as if by magic.

Justice Albie Sachs, of South Africa's Constitutional Court, gave me a copy of a paper he had written discussing his country's TRC in which he argued "the process has created such a powerful and intense moral climate that it wipes out any possibility of denial. Even the most right-wing newspapers always start their editorials by saying that we have to acknowledge that terrible things were done in our name. . . . Once that is done, it creates a climate which puts intense moral pressure on those who supported the system of apartheid to change, and to contribute towards change."

Sachs is a man of great dignity who was gravely injured several years ago by a car bomb planted because of his work with the liberation movement. But instead of embittering him, the experience—indeed, the entire recent South African experience—seems to have deepened his already highly developed sense of compassion and has no doubt left him particularly sensitive to evidence of the possibility of change and reconciliation. But I am unconvinced that anything that has occurred has wiped out *any possibility of denial*.

Champions of the TRC, particularly people cast in the mold of Desmond Tutu—holy men and women, largely Christian, who fought the battle for forgiveness and mutual acceptance—see signs of reconciliation all around. But then it is the job of holy men and women to have faith, to believe, as the Bible puts it, in "the substance of things hoped for, the evidence of things not seen." Obviously, by some measures, reconciliation has, and is, taking place, not only in South Africa, but also in the other places discussed above. But exactly to what extent it has taken place depends on how you view reconciliation.

"Reconciliation," writes Sachs, "lies in converting knowledge into acknowledgment of the pain, in hearing the voices of the victims speaking for themselves in their multiple voices, from all sides, from many different quarters, from all the sections of our society who have suffered pain in different ways. It lies in the perpetrators acknowledging however haltingly, in whatever limited way, at least something of what they did. Reconciliation means the nation, and the world, acknowledging that these terrible things happened."

Acknowledgment is indeed a beginning. But acknowledgment of pain without acceptance of responsibility, without some attempt, even if symbolic, to repair the wrong, leaves many self-declared victims wondering, in the manner of Thandi Shezi, whether reconciliation is something of a farce.

Part of the problem in talking about reconciliation of estranged segments of society is that, even considered a segment at a time, society is not a monolith. Some former victims have managed to do much better than others—and are therefore less likely to cling to their bitterness or to nurse their sense of outrage. They are more inclined to be gracious and forgiving of their perpetrators.

"The international community can marvel at President Mandela's ability not to be bitter. But it's helped tremendously by the fact he doesn't live in poverty; he doesn't live in a shack," observed Jody Kollapan, deputy chairperson of the South African Human Rights Commission.

When some members of the former victim class live in mansions and others live in cardboard shacks, reconciliation, as a societywide concept, loses some of its meaning. So let me focus for a moment on reconciliation in microcosm—at the level of an Everett and Carlucci, at the level of a John Sage, whose Bridges to Life takes on the tasks of healing and reconciling one damaged human being at a time.

Sage's work with victims and prisoners has taught him about the power of empathy, about how prisoners listening to victims and victims listening to prisoners can change the lives of both groups for the better. Sometimes they reach a point of profound understanding of what the other has endured. Connie Hilton believes a substantial part of her recovery from being raped and watching her husband's murder is due to the work she has done in Texas prisons with Sage. As she told her story of violation and saw the concern and the tears in the eyes of prisoners, she came to see them in a new light. "I started to look at them as people." And when they apologized for the crimes she had endured, even though they had not committed those specific crimes, "It helped me."

Such encounters show that healing actually can result when victims and perpetrators are brought together. Indeed, much of so-called restorative justice is aimed at achieving that kind of reconciliation at the individual level—through allowing offenders to see the harm their actions have caused and giving them the opportunity to acknowledge the victim's loss and, if possible, to make amends.

In the New Zealand juvenile justice system the practice has been institutionalized. Since 1989, the law has mandated that "unless the public interest requires otherwise, criminal proceedings should not be instituted against a child or young person if there is an alternative means of dealing with the matter." What that means in practice is that the vast majority of first offenders under the age of seventeen never face a jury or cop a plea.

Many of them instead go through a Family Group Conference—a practice inspired by the indigenous Maōri approach to conflict resolution. In a typical FGC a number of people with an interest in the offender—family members, a policeman, the victim, a social worker, a youth advocate, and others—sit in a circle; and guided by a youth justice coordinator, they try to come up with a plan to keep the young person from offending again. In addition to accepting responsibility for what he or she has done, and perhaps performing community service, the young lawbreaker is also expected to provide reparation. "If a wrong is quantifiable, put it right. Repair it," is how Andrew Becroft, New Zealand's principal Youth Court judge, described the practice.

In a Family Group Conference that I sat in on in Auckland, a young woman who had stolen her mother's car produced a formal letter of apology, agreed to pay damages, and promised to attend anger-management classes. She also pledged to do a host of other things to curb her destructive behavior. The next day I sat in a courtroom with Judge Becroft as he reviewed a proposal from a Family Group Conference to have a teenager who had snatched a tourist's purse replace it with a better purse—an Italian designer model.

Roca, a grassroots organization that works with young people in Massachusetts, has experimented with a similar method of reconciliation—so-called peacemaking circles. The process, adapted in part from Canada's aboriginal culture, essentially forces people to listen. Everyone sits around in a circle, but only one person, the one holding the "talking piece"—an eagle feather by tradition, but it can also be some other object—is allowed to talk at a time.

"Through this process people relax and often listen to one another for the first time. . . . The values of the circle encourage participants to speak from the heart, a pathway that often is blocked by many layers of hurt and anger. Young people on the street carry heavy secret burdens of the violence in their lives," observed Carolyn Boyes-Watson, director of the Center for Restorative Justice at Suffolk University and an adviser to Roca. "The circle can be a place of healing for these wounds that run deep in the fabric of the community. In the circle everyone shares some of their own vulnerability—and it is through that process that people who are isolated find connection and begin healing."

Roca used the circle technique with a group of Puerto Rican and Central American gang members. *What were they fighting over?* the staff wanted to know. In the end, those in the circle acknowledged they had no idea why they were feuding. "They shook hands and ended it," reports Roca's Anisha Chablan.

Such sessions are a far cry from the high drama of the formal truth commissions. But at their best and in their essence they capture a large part of what those commissions are trying to do: to put right those wrongs that are quantifiable and reparable; to find a mutually agreeable path to reconciliation.

When I asked South Africa's Hugo van der Merwe what he saw as the primary mission of South Africa's TRC, he replied, "It's about being honest and not telling ourselves lies. I think that's the first issue. We need to know who we are and what we've done. And what we've allowed to have done around us. Or others to do in our name."

Honesty is much more easily attained in a small circle than in a huge national arena. So is trust. There is no place to hide in a circle and no one else to blame. So in small villages, in a small country, such as East Timor, it's sometimes possible for people, in the traditional way, to sit together and work out issues of truth, trust, responsibility, and repair—certainly much more so than in a huge complicated country like America or, for that matter, Iraq.

But even for a place like East Timor, as Gusmao and Guterres Lopes make clear, reconciliation, in a meaningful national sense, means much more than villagers welcoming former neighbors back to the village they tried to destroy. By the same token, in a place like South Africa, it means more than creating a magical moment when former enemies weep and embrace. It is also about transformation. And, in that, there are certainly parallels between the personal and the global.

The errant teenager sits in a circle with her mother and various officers of the state and pledges to undergo a program of transformation; and the mother, motivated by love and hope, accepts her daughter into her life again. The murderer and the father of the murdered learn to trust each other; the murderer is transformed and a friendship is forged. In the same way that reconciliation in such personal matters can hinge on the promise of transformation, so too can reconciliation of those who feel estranged from their own society. Eduardo González, in other words, had it right: *Reconciliation means to build a different society.*

It means to build a society in which people once excluded feel empowered, in which those once impoverished have a future, in which the values that created the alienation in the first place are no longer the governing norms of a nation but are a memory of how things used to be before the age of awareness arrived.

5.

DISCHARGING A DEBT

WHAT IS THE DEBT FOR THE HOLOCAUST? What is the value of lives lost to slavery? How much do you pay for a "disappeared" father or son? Do you pay as much for one lost family member as for two—as much for a crippling injury as for a death? How much are the bones of your murdered loved one worth? And what about torture? Do you pay for the nightmares that never go away? Do you compensate—or try to compensate— survivors for losses and injustices that span generations, for losses that, in their full dimension, may never be known?

The very effort to place a value on such things as genocide and torture strikes some as sickeningly offensive. "I felt reluctant to define the greatest tragedy in Jewish history in terms of money," wrote Elie Wiesel in his foreword to *Imperfect Justice,* explaining his refusal to preside over the Swiss government's fund for Jewish Holocaust survivors.

Yet, increasingly, lawyers and others who claim to speak for aggrieved persons are attaching numbers—or demanding that numbers be attached—to such things. As governments and corporations are called to make amends for the sins of the past, reparations are routinely being sought as part of the process of apology and atonement. For though money could never repay the pain suffered by survivors of concentration camps or of attempted genocide, it can at least provide an acknowledgment that a wrong was committed and that somebody ought to pay a price.

On my desk is a press release from a leading Roma (or Gypsy) rights organization trumpeting one of "the most significant Roma rights victories to date." That victory concerns a decision by the government of Montenegro to pay 985,000 euros, about $1.13 million, to seventy-four Romani victims of a 1995 vigilante attack.

The mob attacked and destroyed the Romani settlement in Bozova Glavica, Danilovgrad, after allegations that two Romani youths had raped a non-Romani girl. The decision to pay the victims of the so-called Danilovgrad pogrom "restores the dignity of the victims of this terrible crime. In addition, this case must also serve as an example to other countries in the region where numerous Romani victims are yet to obtain redress for abuse suffered," commented Branimir Plese, an attorney for the European Roma Rights Center, one of the groups representing the victims.

It's not just the Roma who are seeking redress. Koreans forced into prostitution as "comfort women" during World War II by the Japanese have repeatedly demanded an apology and reparations from the Japanese government. Members of the "stolen generation"—the tens of thousands of Australian aboriginals taken from their parents in a misguided effort at assimilation—have demanded that Australia pay for the trauma and cultural isolation they endured. "The reparation we are seeking will aim to help heal the wounds resulting from government initiated forced removal policies. The losses are many and deep. It includes loss of identity, culture, language, loss of our land and cultural community. Funding from a Reparations Tribunal will help Stolen Generations return to visit country and connect with community. It will also provide personal counseling to those who have not been able to commence their healing. . . . It will also enable nonindigenous Australians to leave behind their guilt. Only then can we move forward together as a Nation," declared Audrey Ngingali Kinnear, cochair of the National Sorry Day Committee, at a 2001 reparations conference in Australia. Some Armenians are no less passionate in their belief that reparations are owed for the Armenian massacre of 1915. In an editorial published online in 2002, the *Armenian Weekly* passionately called for the world to recognize—and for Turkey to pay for—the Armenian massacre of 1915. Various countries and Swiss banks had already coughed up restitution for Jews who were cheated and abused during the Holocaust, noted the editorial, which concluded, "Turkey must also pay for its crimes."

How strong of a claim could the current generation have for wrongs committed an eon ago? To what extent can a nation even pay such debts? And what happens if one tries?

Those questions ultimately led me to New Zealand, where a document signed in 1840 called The Treaty of Waitangi has become the focal point of a struggle for redress of offenses that span generations.

That treaty was negotiated by William Hobson who, as agent to Her Majesty Queen Victoria, had been instructed to obtain land "by fair and equal contracts." Some 500 Maōri chiefs signed the treaty, which guaranteed the Maōri control in perpetuity over their lands—or so they apparently thought—but yielded sovereignty, or governance, to the people they called Pākehā.

Article the first: *Chiefs of the Confederation of the United Tribes of New Zealand and the separate and independent Chiefs who have not become members of the Confederation, cede to Her Majesty the Queen of England, absolutely and without reservation, all the rights and power of Sovereignty which the said Confederation or Individual Chiefs respectively exercise or possess, or may be supposed to exercise or to possess over their respective Territories as the sole Sovereigns thereof.*

Article the second: *Her Majesty the Queen of England confirms and guarantees to the Chiefs and Tribes of New Zealand and to the respective families and individuals thereof, the full exclusive possession of the Lands and Estates, Forest, Fisheries, and other properties which they may collectively or individually possess, so long as it is their wish and desire to maintain the same in their possession; but the Chiefs of the United Tribes and the Individual Chiefs yield to Her Majesty the exclusive right of Preemption over such lands as the proprietors thereof may be disposed to alienate, at such prices as may be agreed upon between the respective proprietors and persons appointed by Her Majesty to treat with them in that behalf.*

Since most of the Maōri leaders spoke no English, a Maōri translation of the treaty was provided. That translation was flawed. The Maōri version translated *sovereignty* with a word *(kāwanatanga)* that Maōri leaders don't equate with sovereignty or anything approximating total control. They thought—or so scholars now claim—that they were merely agreeing that the English could govern the people who settled on the land.

In subsequent years, the settlers, in effect, ignored the Maōri interpretation. There were wars, widespread confiscation of lands, and peaceful protests; but the English interpretation prevailed. Then the 1960s rolled around, along with a worldwide human rights revolution; and there was a stirring of Maōri anger and pride. The Maōri demanded that their language be taught in schools and that their culture be respected. In 1974, Matiu Rata, minister of Maōri affairs, introduced a bill seeking adherence to Treaty of Waitangi obligations. That bill went nowhere; but the next year Whina Cooper, the revered elderly daughter of a Maōri chief, led a history-making thousand-plus kilometer trek from the North Island to the Parliament. Tens of thousands accompanied her, demanding that the government honor the treaty, that the government give the Maōri their due, that the government stop taking Maōri land.

The growing anger and awareness among the Maōri forced politicians to act. If the government did nothing, they feared, there would be "not just racial disharmony, but acts of civil disobedience, leading to bloodshed," recalls John Tamihere, a Maōri and a member of Parliament.

The Maōri movement spawned the Waitangi Tribunal: a "permanent commission of inquiry." From its perch in the capital of Wellington, the Tribunal began the work of trying to correct treaty violations. Initially, the Tribunal could only look at claims that arose in modern times—beginning with 1975, the year the bill creating the Tribunal was passed. But in 1985, the Tribunal's scope was dramatically expanded. It was given power to look into claims stretching all the way back to 1840. The Tribunal cannot actually hand over land or other resources; it can only facilitate and recommend. But those recommendations are taken seriously. So the Tribunal has become the symbol, and also the principal instrument, of an astonishing change in New Zealand society. In its attempt to repair the acts of the early settlers and their descendants, New Zealand is transferring hundreds of millions of dollars—along with fishing rights and other valuable resources—to Maōri tribes.

That transfer has provoked controversy and grumbling among Maōri and non-Maōri alike. *Is the money being spent wisely?* critics ask. *Are the right people in control?*

One of the largest settlements, some $170 million and a substantial quantity of land, was won by the Tainui tribe. The tribe also received an apology from the Crown for the confiscation of its land. Subsequently, to the huge embarrassment of the Tainui Confederation, it came out that the tribe had lost millions on a rugby team, which it finally sold. Other money-losing ventures also came to light.

The scandal provoked endless discussion, angry charges of financial mismanagement, and widespread rumors of Tainui's impending financial collapse. A heated 2001 editorial from the

New Zealand Herald fumed over the secrecy of Maōri leaders unwilling to discuss the dispensation of Treaty of Waitangi funds. And it lambasted Tainui—the "settlement trail-blazer"—for its inability, over six years, to add value to the $170 million settlement it had received in 1995. The *Herald* saw Tainui's humiliation as something of a lesson in the folly of hubris. Tribal leaders "lost sight of the fact that every member of Tainui—and succeeding generations—should benefit from the settlement." The *Herald* was particularly scornful of the decision to invest in the Warriors rugby league team, a decision that "suggested . . . personal pride was a more powerful motivator than tribal welfare."

Ironically, under new ownership, the rugby team reversed its fortunes. The Tainui Confederation also improved its financial performance. But questions about the money linger. On what should it be spent? To whom does it really belong? And what, ultimately, is it meant to accomplish?

For Neville Baker, acting director of the Waitangi Tribunal, the answer to the last question is clear. The point of the Tribunal and of the settlements is not simply to provide people with money; it's also about something much more profound: "what gives you back your dignity, or your *mana.*" It's about people finding "some relief" as they see various wrongs of the past "now wiped clean." It's also about acknowledging a painful reality: "Had the treaty been honored when it was signed, we would not have half of the problems we have today."

The problems to which he refers are reflected in statistics that show that by any measure of socioeconomic well-being, from educational attainment to rate of incarceration, Maōri are significantly less well off than Pākehā.

"For whatever reason, Maōris are not progressing in education," said Baker. "Education is probably the key to change for the Maōri." He also observed that, for several generations, New Zealand had made substantial investments in "negative options," most notably in prisons. A new prison, he pointed out, was going up in a heavily Maōri area of "high unemployment, poor education, low opportunity." That prison, he said, reflected the assumption that large numbers of Maōri would be incarcerated in the next several years. Locking them up near their homes would make it easier for families to visit them. "It is an indictment of this country . . . to deliver a message like this to a Maōri community and say that is where your future is going to be," railed Baker.

What did any of that have to do with the work of the Tribunal? Ideally, the Tribunal's work would contribute to the odds of success for the next generation; it would help to keep people out of jail.

Tribunal member Ann Parsoson said she found the settlement process "intensely emotional." When tribal representatives got together to receive an acknowledgment and apology on behalf of the Crown, there was "a tremendous feeling involved," a sense that someone was finally being "held to account." Finally people had a tangible acknowledgment that their problems did not fully reside in themselves: "Sometimes it releases people from the feeling that it's their own inadequacies" that had left so many Maōri impoverished and marginalized.

Baker confided that he was the youngest of twelve children and at sixty-three, the only one surviving. His mother had been unable to read. He was one of only two of the children to go to school. He was a member, in a sense, of a transitional generation, a generation that had protested against Pākehā ways and Pākehā outrages but had not, until relatively recently, seen much in the way of change. "People said if we're not going to be successful in protests against all these things, we need to get educated."

He was also a member of the generation that witnessed the return from World War II of the highly decorated soldiers from the celebrated Maōri battalion. Those soldiers were proud, fearless fighters who—like their Maōri counterparts during World War I—showed that Maōri were every bit as effective in combat as were Europeans. But it was a lesson taught at a price. From one community, he noted, some twenty-four Maōri went off to war—they were the most highly educated and highly motivated of all—and only one came back. "We probably lost most of our leadership, most of our talent," he said. Those who spoke the best English, who were most capable of confronting the New Zealand government, were disproportionately among those lost in combat.

Baker, of course, was making a point: His people have sacrificed and suffered greatly, and they have been waiting a long, long time for some of the wrongs of history to be corrected. "Unless you deal with some of the grievances of the past and do it in a way that brings out the truth," he said, "it will be difficult for a country to go on."

How long would the settlement of grievances take? Baker said the goal was to finish the process by the year 2010, but that goal would probably not be met. There were many claims, and the office had not nearly enough resources. And there was also the distraction of having to justify what the Tribunal was doing: "There are people in New Zealand who don't think the Tribunal should exist, who think the Maōri are overly pandered to and the settlements are extravagant. . . . We're under attack a lot of the time."

Mahara Okeroa, a member of Parliament and chair of the Maōri affairs select committee, saw the settlements as an important—but not sufficient—remedy for the problems that bedevil the Maōri. "It takes more than a package of money and a package of apologies," he said. Plus the money, he pointed out, amounted to only a fraction of a percent of the value of the confiscated lands. "Our people are being forced to settle for it," he said. So some simply shrugged and essentially said, "We've got something, let's move on."

John Tamihere, minister of youth affairs, minister of statistics, associate minister of Maōri affairs, Labour Party member, and a rising star in Parliament, sees the Treaty of Waitangi as a seminal and vital document. "That treaty is our Magna Carta, our Declaration of Independence."

A handsome, clean-shaven lawyer in his forties, Tamihere is both warm and forceful. He welcomes a stranger into his home by gathering his wife and older son around him and singing a traditional Maōri welcome song. But though he venerates tradition, he is not afraid to take on his elders—some of whom, he believes, have not recognized that things have fundamentally changed since the old days, a time when Maōri lived far from the city with their respective tribes.

In 1956, he says, some 86 percent of the Maōri lived in rural areas; but the population shifted. Twenty years later, the majority lived in cities. At present, he estimated, eight out of ten Maōri in New Zealand no longer live with their tribes. Yet for the most part settlements based on the Treaty of Waitangi are controlled by tribal leaders. "My fear is that we will build a brown aristocracy. . . . What about the masses?"

The concern, he said, is not merely theoretical. Before entering Parliament, Tamihere headed Te Whānau o Waipareira Trust, an Auckland-based social services organization that provided job training and other assistance to disadvantaged Maōri youths. He asked the leaders of one of the tribal groups that had received a settlement to provide jobs for his young people. They refused, said Tamihere; and he ended up going to court and before the Tribunal to argue that urban Maōri not necessarily connected by tribal ties should benefit from the treaty settlements. The Tribunal ultimately concluded that certain urban Maōri organizations did indeed deserve to be consulted and that the needs of urban Maōri should be taken into account.

Nonetheless, argues Tamihere, tribal leaders routinely give short shrift to those needs. And instead of investing in scholarships, educational programs, jobs, and other activities that would improve the lot of young Maōri, they tend to invest in simple money-making schemes. Nonetheless, they expect other Maōri to accept their leadership.

"The tribal elite say, 'This is our culture.' I say that's bas-

tardized, that's feudalism. And we never practiced feudalism."
Unless that leadership becomes considerably more responsible,
Tamihere predicts "in the next few years there will be great intra-
Maōri fights."

Traditionally, he pointed out, the leaders ate last when food
was served; they first made sure everyone else was fed. But some
of the new tribal elite, he charged, have built "a top table" where
they dine first. Another Maōri professional expressed the same
thought in even more pointed language: "There is the round
table," she said, referring to the leading New Zealand business-
men, "and now there is the brown table."

The Tribunal's Neville Baker emphatically rejected the view
that tribal chiefs had become "fat cats gathering massive settlements." The elders, he pointed out, were respected for their ability
to make wise decisions. Tamihere, he observed, was a "politician
not afraid to capitalize on saying things that will put him on the
front page."

Nonetheless, Tamihere's central concern is undeniably relevant—not only to the disposition of settlements in New Zealand,
but to any group seeking redress in the form of resources for the
wrongs of the past. How should those resources be distributed?
Who should make the decisions? Is the goal simply to get adherence to the law or to the essence of an ancient commitment? If
chiefs signed a treaty in the old days, then are the chiefs of today
the only parties that need be answered to? Or is the goal to provide some form of uplift for an entire community? And how do
you compensate for the fact that the problems and the characteris-
tics of the relevant population today are radically different from
what they were yesterday? Baker is very likely right when he
asserts that many problems would not exist had the treaty been
honored when it was signed. But that's a bit like saying that
America's race problem would not exist if people had never been
enslaved. Or the Holocaust might have been averted had the
Nazis been prevented from coming to power. Since the treaty

wasn't honored, since enslavement and the Holocaust did happen, the only real questions concern how and to what extent things can be set right.

No amount of compensation can put things back to where they should have been—not that anyone is prepared to offer infinite sums to do so. But is that even the point of reparations? Are they supposed to somehow make up for the past? Or do they have some grander purpose? The Maōri are not the only group wrestling with such questions. They arise whenever the topic of reparations is discussed, wherever cash is demanded for the mixture of moral and economic wrongs that leave devastated or damaged victims in their wake.

No victims are more noted, of course, than Jewish survivors of the Holocaust. In the years following World War II, a defeated and yet, in some respects, defiant Germany was called to account for at least some of its sins. As Christian Pross observed in *Paying for the Past:* "The German people did not like the victims, and they certainly did not like paying for them." Reparations were forced on a reluctant Germany by the Allies, the state of Israel, and by groups who claimed to speak directly for the victims of the horrors of the so-called final solution—most notably the Conference on Jewish Material Claims Against Germany and the United Restitution Organization.

In an address to the Bundestag in September 1951, Chancellor Konrad Adenauer of West Germany acknowledged Germany's obligation to do something of substance for Jewish survivors: "The overwhelming majority of the German people abhorred the crimes committed against the Jews and were not involved in them. . . . However, unspeakable crimes were committed in the name of the German people, which create a duty of moral and material reparations."

Following a difficult series of negotiations, a deal was struck in Luxembourg the following year whereby Germany agreed to pay 3.5 billion deutsch marks in reparations, of which 3 billion would go to Israel, where some half million refugees had fled during the war and immediately thereafter. The rest would be distributed by the Conference on Jewish Material Claims Against Germany, which represented those Holocaust victims outside of Israel. The payments were to go to individual victims of Nazi persecution as well as those whose property had been confiscated, destroyed, or unfairly acquired. Funds were also to go for rehabilitation and resettlement of Jews and toward the rebuilding of communities and institutions destroyed by the Nazis.

The Luxembourg treaty agreement encountered substantial resistance in the Bundestag, but it was ratified in 1953. In subsequent years, additional reparations agreements were reached with the German and Austrian governments, who were shamed and cajoled into increasing the ante. "The Federal Republic did not pay reparations out of a sense of moral responsibility, but above all for political reasons," concluded Pross, who estimated the total reparations payments by the year 2000 at over 100 billion deutsch marks, or nearly $60 billion.

In the 1990s, yet another avenue for Holocaust reparations opened up. In 1992 the World Jewish Congress mobilized, establishing the World Jewish Restitution Organization to recover Jewish assets appropriated in Europe. American lawyers and politicians quickly and energetically took up the fight. They accused the Swiss National Bank of Holocaust profiteering—or, as put by Stuart Eizenstat in *Imperfect Justice,* of being the "principle money changer for the Third Reich." They charged the bankers with three specific crimes: confiscating the deposits of Holocaust-era Jewish clients; receiving assets looted by the Nazis; and profiting from slave labor. For over fifty years, the banks had gotten away with such crimes, but as the Swiss discovered, things had changed substantially since the end of World War II. Not only had American courts become much more receptive to international claims rooted in human rights law, but the political environment was also very different from what it had been in previous decades—a point made by Michael Bazyler in a 2002 article in the *Berkeley Journal of International Law:*

> *First, beginning in April 1996, the U.S. Senate Banking Committee, headed by Senator Alfonse D'Amato, held hearings on the issue. Second, a number of state and local governments threatened to stop doing business with the Swiss banks unless they settled the claims. Third, in May 1997, the United States government issued a report, written by then-Undersecretary of State Stuart Eizenstat (and later Deputy Treasury Secretary and Special Representative of the President and the Secretary of State for Holocaust Issues) sharply criticizing the Swiss for their World War II dealings with the Nazis. Finally, UBS [Union Banks of Switzerland], now undergoing a merger with co-defendant Swiss Bank Corporation, was caught attempting to shred World War II–era financial documents, in violation of a newly enacted Swiss law forbidding such actions.*

Authors John Authers and Richard Wolffe suggest that the time was also ripe economically. "With economies booming across the world in the late 1990s, there was a critical window of opportunity for settling the issue of Holocaust profits once and for all," they noted in *The Victim's Fortune.* Also, since the Cold War was over, the United States was less reluctant than previously to confront its allies.

Originally, the main action was at the negotiating table—with the Swiss banks and the Swiss government on one side and the World Jewish Restitution Organization and the American presidency, represented by Stuart Eizenstat, on the other. But then, to use Eizenstat's phrase, "The lawyers hijacked the Swiss bank dispute."

Their weapon was the class action suit. Those suits, and the unyielding political and diplomatic pressure, forced the banks and Swiss industries in 1998 to agree to cough up $1.25 billion. The amount was hardly the result of a precise calculation of damages. It was impossible, for one thing, in most cases, to link specific victims to looted assets or profits. The figure was essentially a compromise located between figures the opposing sides picked out of the air—an approximation of the amount needed to provide some small degree of "rough justice." In short order, banks and industries in other countries also yielded to demands for restitution. The Germans agreed to $5 billion; the French and Austrians to lesser amounts. The total—and not all of it was for Jews; a small amount was earmarked for the Roma, the handicapped, and other victimized groups—eventually climbed to upwards of $8 billion.

As Eizenstat acknowledges, there was less than universal satisfaction with this "final accounting" for the horrors of the Holocaust. "Obviously it was too late for those who were killed during the war or died in the years afterward. There were also real costs to our enterprise. Critics, even in the Jewish community, charged that the emphasis on material restitution overshadowed the human tragedy of the Holocaust. Others railed against what they saw as an insidious 'Holocaust industry' of lawyers and Jewish organizations profiting at the expense of victims." There were also victims such as Simon Rozenkier, a Polish native used as a guinea pig by demented Nazi scientists. Complaining that the paltry sum offered through the settlement was not nearly enough to cover the loss and pain, Rosenkier sued two German pharmaceutical companies in 2003 in an attempt to collect more.

Nor, points out Eizenstat, was there any easy moral lesson. There had been no sudden recognition of moral wrongs. Instead legal, political, and economic pressure has forced those targeted to capitulate. "The cost of fighting cases they might have won in a court of law had become too steep to sustain in the court of public opinion and in the enormous, profitable U.S. marketplace," wrote Eizenstat. If there was a great lesson, he believed, it had to do with the irrepressibility of truth: "Historical facts can be suppressed, but eventually they bubble to the surface."

The truth of what happened to Japanese Americans during World War II was never much in dispute. Some 120,000 were arrested in 1942 and held in concentration camps, supposedly in the national interest. Supreme Court Associate Justice William O. Douglas, concurring in *Kiyoshi Hirabayashi v. U.S.,* 1943., bluntly made the case:

> *After the disastrous bombing of Pearl Harbor the military had a grave problem on its hands. The threat of Japanese invasion of the west coast was not fanciful but real. The presence of many thousands of aliens and citizens of Japanese ancestry in or near to the key points along that coastline aroused special concern in those charged with the defense of the country. . . . If the military were right in their belief that among citizens of Japanese ancestry there was an actual or incipient fifth column, we were indeed faced with the imminent threat of a dire emergency. We must credit the military with as much good faith in that belief as we would any other public official acting pursuant to his duties. We cannot possibly know all the facts which lay behind that decision.*

As the war wound down, the country realized its mistake. In December 1944, with a Supreme Court decision on the question pending, the military reversed itself and declared that detainees, as of January 1945, could return home. The last of the camps was shut down in 1946. But nearly half a century elapsed before the U.S. Congress made amends.

Like the Holocaust victims and the Maōri treaty claimants, the Japanese Americans benefited from a change in attitude and from the rise of a human rights culture. They also benefited from the civil rights movement, which as Mitchell Maki *et al.* observed in *Achieving the Impossible Dream,* "taught the lessons, provided the energy, and instilled the inspiration through which the modern redress struggle emerged."

Throughout the 1970s, as activists made the case to various

constituencies, support grew for the idea of restitution. Yvonne Braithwaite Burke, chair of the Congressional Black Caucus, pledged her support to the efforts in 1975. The Japanese American Citizens League announced its Reparations Campaign Committee the following year.

Rather than pursue reparations directly, advocates and their congressional allies decided to proceed in stages. They came up with legislation to create a Commission on Wartime Relocation and Internment of Civilians to study the issue. The legislation passed in 1980, and President Jimmy Carter signed it into law. The commission's report, issued in February 1983, was an indictment of U.S. treatment of Japanese Americans during the war:

> *This policy of exclusion, removal and detention was executed against 120,000 people without individual review, and exclusion was continued virtually without regard for their demonstrated loyalty to the United States. . . .*
>
> *All this was done despite the fact that not a single documented act of espionage, sabotage or fifth column activity was committed by an American citizen of Japanese ancestry or by a resident Japanese alien on the West Coast. . . .*
>
> *The broad historical causes which shaped these decisions were race prejudice, war hysteria and a failure of political leadership. Widespread ignorance of Japanese-Americans contributed to a policy conceived in haste and executed in an atmosphere of fear and anger at Japan.*
>
> *A grave injustice was done to American citizens and resident aliens of Japanese ancestry who, without individual review or any probative evidence against them, were excluded, removed and detained by the United States during World War II.*

Payments began in October 1990 at an emotionally charged ceremony, featuring Attorney General Richard Thornburgh, in the Great Hall of Justice.

"By finally admitting a wrong, a nation does not destroy its integrity, but rather reinforces the sincerity of its commitment to the Constitution, and hence to its people. In forcing us to reexamine our history, you have made us only stronger and more proud," declared Thornburgh at the ceremony as he handed out $20,000 checks and a letter of apology from President George Bush.

There was "more than a tinge of irony to the letters—and a special urgency to yesterday's ceremony," wrote *Washington Post* reporter Michael Isikoff, who went on to observe: "Since President Ronald Reagan signed the law more than two years ago, funding for the reparations has wound slowly through the congressional appropriations process and money became available only with the start of the new fiscal year last week. In the meantime, 1,600 survivors of the camps have died and thousands more are ailing, unable to enjoy the funds they are slated to receive."

Congressman Robert Matsui, who was six months old when he was interned along with his parents, believes the process that led to the payment of reparations was beneficial in itself. "There was . . . a catharsis in the community that grew from the very process of strategizing the redress legislation and seeing it through to fruition. Japanese Americans in their sixties, seventies, and eighties and some even older—many of whom had never voted—got involved in testifying, letter writing, and lobbying. Many of them had never been able to talk about their agonizing experiences, even with one another, let alone air their pain in public," wrote Matsui in the foreword to *Achieving the Impossible Dream*.

Matsui also confided that he had only realized as an adult that he still carried scars from his incarceration—scars that cut to the core of his being, scars that as a child had made him ashamed to acknowledge what his family had endured. He saw the restitution, and the acknowledgment and apology that came with it, as society's way of "liberating future generations" from the trauma and shame that he had borne.

Survivors of another American tragedy, similarly shrouded in silence, have recently told their story to the world. But unlike the story of Japanese internment, which was widely known and always recognized as part of the chronicle of World War II, the tragedy that struck Tulsa, Oklahoma, was until recently largely unknown. That incident had been swept into a corner of historical neglect and lost in the muddle of misremembered things to which shameful episodes are so often consigned.

Thanks to a recent bounty of articles and books, and a formal investigation by the Oklahoma Commission to Study the Tulsa Race Riot of 1921, the major facts are no longer in question. On the morning of May 31, 1921, Tulsa had a thriving black community called Greenwood—a community so prosperous that it was known as the Black Wall Street of America, one of the few places in America where blacks could dream of success on a grand scale. By the time the sun went down the following evening, Black Wall Street was a smoldering mass of burned-out houses, dead bodies, and devastated dreams. Between seventy-five and three hundred people were killed; the true number will probably never be known because of the cover-up that followed. More than one thousand homes were razed. "A mob destroyed thirty-five-square blocks of the African-American community during the evening of May 31, through the afternoon of June 1, 1921. It was a tragic, infamous moment in Oklahoma and the nation's history. The worst civil disturbance since the Civil War," wrote State Representative Don Ross in the Tulsa riot commission report.

For years, the episode was essentially forgotten, left out of America's history books and purged from the nation's collective memory, not so much out of shame but because, from the perspective of white Tulsa, it was all so unseemly—and so bad for the city's image.

The series of events began with an apparently bogus complaint that a black man had attempted to assault a white woman in an elevator. The young man was arrested and an inflammatory newspaper article appeared. "Negro Assaults a White Girl!" was the headline. Perhaps there was also an angry editorial. It remains unclear if the editorial, supposedly headlined "To Lynch a Negro Tonight," was actually published, since the editorials from that day's *Tulsa Tribune,* presumably in a bid to salvage the paper's reputation, were systematically destroyed.

Mobilized by reports of the assault, whites showed up outside the jail en masse, amid much talk of lynching. Armed blacks, fearful that yet another lynching was about to take place, headed downtown, intent on protecting the young man in custody. The sheriff pledged not to give the man to the mob and convinced the anxious blacks to return home. The whites, incensed at the blacks' temerity in coming downtown *armed no less,* worked themselves into a frenzy. They grabbed whatever weapons they could find. Some broke into and raided gun shops. Armed with rifles, shotguns, pistols, kerosene, even machine guns, and fueled by liquor and rage, they laid siege to Greenwood. The National Guard was called in and became the rioters' military auxiliary. At one point airplanes appeared in the sky. As James Hirsch reported in *Riot and Remembrance:*

> *Exactly what they did has been debated ever since but numerous black witnesses have said the aircraft were used to assault Greenwood: pilots either dropped incendiary devices like "turpentine balls" and dynamite or used rifles to strafe people from the sky. If true, Tulsa was the first U.S. city to suffer an aerial assault. But police officials say the planes were used only to monitor the fires and to locate refugees. . . . Even if the planes were not used for offensive purposes, their presence emphasized the total-war atmosphere of the raid and seared another harrowing image into many blacks' memories.*

Greenwood's residents fought heroically to save their homes; but they never stood a chance. The mob burned their community to the ground. As Tim Madigan reported in *The Burning,* "Panoramic photographs of the decimation bore a haunting resemblance to those from Nagasaki and Hiroshima a quarter-century later: Thirty-five square blocks of the Negro community lay almost completely in ruin, save for hundreds of outhouses and a few isolated residences. As the whites had moved north on June 1, they put the torch to more than 1,115 Negro homes (314 more were looted, but not burned), five hotels, thirty-one restaurants, four drugstores, eight doctors' offices, the new Dunbar School, two dozen grocery stores, the Negro hospital, the public library, and even a dozen churches, including the community's most magnificent new edifice, Mount Zion Baptist Church." And later, when the smoke cleared, city officials charged the blacks with inciting the riot.

Subsequently, black property owners filed some $4 million in claims. All were denied. Over a hundred lawsuits filed by blacks following the disturbance were also dismissed by Oklahoma courts. Nothing was provided for the destruction of the community, though the city did approve two claims exceeding $5,000 to white gun shop owners for ammunition and weaponry stolen in the heat of the riot.

The cover-up that followed the massacre is almost as mind-boggling as the riot itself. For much of Oklahoma, life quickly went back to normal. People pretended the upheaval had never happened; and over time most people convinced themselves that it had not. When the riot commission's report was released in February 2001, there was a sense that Tulsa was finally ready to acknowledge what had happened and to make appropriate amends. The report itself contained an unabashed endorsement of reparations.

"The riot proclaimed that there were two Oklahomas; that one claimed the right to push down, push out, and push under the other; and that it had the power to do so," proclaimed the report, before delivering the kicker to the sermon:

That is what the Tulsa race riot has been all about for so long afterwards, why it has lingered not as a past event but lived as a

present entity. It kept on saying that there remained two Okla-
homas; that one claimed the right to be dismissive of, ignorant
of, and oblivious to the other; and that it had the power to do
that.

That is why the Tulsa race riot can be about something else. It
can be about making two Oklahomas one—but only if we un-
derstand that this is what reparation is all about. Because the riot
is both symbolic and singular, reparations become both singular
and symbolic, too. Compelled not legally by courts but extended
freely by choice, they say that individual acts of reparation will
stand as symbols that fully acknowledge and finally discharge a
collective responsibility.

Because we must face it: There is no way but by government
to represent the collective, and there is no way but by reparations
to make real the responsibility.

Does this commission have specific recommendations about
whether or not reparations can or should be made and the appro-
priate methods? Yes, it surely does. . . .

Reparations are the right thing to do.

In the prologue he penned to the commission's report, Ross was
even more forceful:

There was murder, false imprisonment, forced labor, a cover-up,
and local precedence for restitution. . . . The preponderance of the
information demands what was promised. Whether it was Ku
Klux Klan instigated, land speculators' conspiracy, inspired by
yellow journalism, or random acts, it happened. Justice demands a
closure as it did with Japanese Americans and Holocaust victims
of Germany. It is a moral obligation. Tulsa was likely the first city
in the [nation] to be bombed from the air. There was a precedent
of payments to at least two white victims of the riot. The issue
today is what government entity should provide financial repair to
the survivors and the condemned community that suffered under

vigilante violence? The Report tells the story, let justice point the
finger and begin the reconciliation!

In *Riot and Remembrance,* published in 2002, author James
Hirsch anticipated a happy ending. He congratulated the city on
breaking the "culture of silence" and called Tulsa "a model of how
a city sought redemption."

Not quite. Not yet.

As I write these words, in August 2003, survivors of the Tulsa
riot and descendants who lost property have filed a lawsuit against
the State of Oklahoma, the City of Tulsa, Tulsa's Police Department, and Tulsa's police chief. They hope that lawsuit will win
them the compensation the city and state did not see fit to pay. The
lawyers' complaint takes note of the recommendations of the commission and of the widespread expectation that those recommendations would be followed: "Instead, it appears that despite the
concurrence in and acknowledgment of the facts establishing their
complicity in the Riot and its consequences, the state and munici-
pality have decided to wait for the survivors, all of them in excess of
eighty years old, to die off so that the problem will 'silently' pass
away."

Don Ross, the state representative who was instrumental in the
creation of the riot commission, retired in 2002, after twenty years
in the state legislature. When we spoke in July 2003, he was not at
all happy with how things had turned out. The city, he said, had
dug in its heels "and the prevailing attitude about the riot is as it
was in 1921—to ignore it, for it to go away, to do nothing." He
was once hopeful that things would not be so, that there would, at
the very least, be a memorial museum commemorating the losses
of the riot. There was even a bond issue that he thought might
fund the museum. But that was before lawmakers relying on
polling data decided that the public—at least the white public—
was not particularly in favor of the idea. He accuses the city of
using the threat of the survivors' lawsuit as an excuse for digging

in: "There's no positive sign that anything's going to be done. . . . I saw [the commission report] as a way to bring the two communities together." But Tulsa, as he sees it, responded with: "We won't give them anything."

Michael Hausfeld, a partner in the Washington law firm Cohen, Milstein, Hausfeld & Toll, is working with an array of lawyers—most notably Charles Ogletree, a famous civil rights and defense attorney who teaches at Harvard Law School—to make sure that "We won't" is not Tulsa's final answer. Compact, balding, with wire-rimmed glasses, Hausfeld projects intensity and intelligence. The suit against Tulsa and Oklahoma, he acknowledged, faced "formidable legal obstacles." The statute of limitations, in particular, would be difficult to get around.

Such statutes are designed to ensure that people don't do precisely what Hausfeld had done: walk into court with a claim decades after the fact when memories have faded, witnesses have died, and the likelihood of establishing liability is all but nil. Nonetheless, Hausfeld felt there were compelling reasons—just as there were with the Holocaust restitution cases—that the claims should go forward.

The essence of the argument is that Oklahoma was not disposed to entertain such suits from blacks at the time the suits ideally should have been filed. The black community well understood the futility of trying to fight the system in the 1920s. How could they expect justice from a grand jury that had already blamed "bad Negroes" for the riot, a grand jury that was on record ridiculing in racist language the idea that Negroes had the same rights as whites? It would have been not only futile to argue the case back then but also dangerous. "The entire community had been obliterated." There could not possibly have been a more hostile or "intimidating environment." In the wake of the massacre, the victims were understandably not particularly inclined to try to exercise their supposed—yet elusive—rights, certainly not before the very people and institutions that had just tried to destroy them.

They were more concerned with trying to pull their lives together as they sought safety in invisibility.

Even those who had the faith and the courage to bring claims, argued Hausfeld, faced yet another hurdle: "fraudulent concealment." There was a wholesale cover-up on the part of the state, a decision to destroy, deny, or tamper with the evidence claimants would need to wage a successful legal fight.

Hausfeld had yet another argument for why the statute of limitation should not apply: "With mass tragedies, time gives you more information, not less." The Greenwood massacre was not just a random, violent incident; it was the destruction of an entire community, of a culture, of a way of life. Such a titanic trauma could not be assessed as if it were some ordinary event. Memories did not necessarily fade over time. Nor did evidence evaporate. Indeed, history brought a certain clarity and perspective to such atrocities. So the very rationale for the statute of limitations became significantly less compelling when confronted with the reality of a Greenwood.

Hausfeld was confident the legal arguments were strong; he was less certain about the political will to do right. He found it strange and disturbing that, even when faced with a suit, Tulsa was dragging its heels. "No one has sat down with us to say, 'What do you really want?'" Hausfeld said, just before he hopped on a plane to Tulsa in late summer 2003.

Oklahoma's response was in stark contrast to that of Florida, which also saw a black community destroyed by a frenzied white mob. A small all-black town of about two hundred people in north Florida, Rosewood was attacked in January 1923 after (what else?) an unidentified black man supposedly sexually assaulted a white woman. Not only were several residents killed, but the community was also totally destroyed. The homes were torched, property was stolen, and the inhabitants were chased into the wilderness. Following the rampage, Rosewood's black residents disappeared,

leaving their burned-out homes and land behind. As in Tulsa, officials found no reason to prosecute any rioters. And, as in Tulsa, the
entire shameful episode was forgotten as Rosewood, already
destroyed, literally vanished from history—until 1982, when a
reporter for the *St. Petersburg Times* stumbled upon the story. The
resulting article spurred some national notice. And a decade later a
group of survivors approached the state legislature, demanding a
memorial and restitution.

The story of a vengeance-crazed white mob destroying a black
town struck many Floridians as an outrageous fabrication. The legislature commissioned a study from a team of researchers at Florida
universities to get to the truth. That report, released in December
1993, was a hard-hitting denunciation of Florida officials and an
unabashed brief for the Rosewood survivors:

> *We believe that Sheriff Walker failed to control local events and
> to request proper assistance from Governor Hardee when events
> moved beyond his control. While Hardee condemned the violence
> and ordered a special prosecutor to conduct a grand jury investi-
> gation, he did so (more than a month had passed) only after black
> residents were forced to leave Rosewood and their property was
> destroyed.*
>
> *The failure of elected white officials to take forceful actions to
> protect the safety and property of local black residents was part of
> a pattern in the state and throughout the region. . . .*
>
> *Like the racial violence in Ocoee, Perry and numerous other
> communities throughout Florida and the South during this era,
> Rosewood was a tragedy of American democracy and the Ameri-
> can legal system. In all these incidents, alleged assaults against
> white women were sufficient to warrant the abandonment of the
> American justice system. The need to protect southern white
> women was seen as sufficient to justify racial violence and op-
> pression. When black resistance was added to an alleged assault*

*upon a white woman then elements of southern society believed
retribution against the entire black community was warranted.
Far too many whites believed an example had to be set so that
other black communities throughout Florida understood that
such resistance to southern racial mores would not be tolerated.
We conclude that by their failure to restrain the mob and to up-
hold the legal due process, the white leaders of the state and country were willing to tolerate such behavior by white citizens.*

With the report in hand, legislators passed the Rosewood
Compensation Act, which provided for scholarships and awarded
nine survivors of the so-called Rosewood massacre $150,000 apiece.
In 1997, director John Singleton released a movie chronicling the
massacre.

As the Rosewood report makes clear, what happened in
Florida and Oklahoma was part of a much larger pattern: the
researchers labeled the event part of a "reign of terror against
African Americans during the period from 1917 to 1923." Few
Americans wanted to admit such a thing was going on at the time,
so whenever possible such violence was glossed over, covered up,
forgotten. Or if that was not possible because the atrocity was so
flagrant, blame was placed on the shoulders of the blacks who
were its victim. *We didn't want to lynch him, but he attacked a white
women. Decency demanded that we respond.* More often than not,
the supposed attack was unproven, uncorroborated, and not credible by normal forensic standards; but mob behavior had a peculiar logic of its own driven by the attitude given voice by a
contemporaneous article in the Gainesville *Daily Sun* that was dug
up by the Rosewood researchers: "One thing, however, we shall
say now—in whatever state it may be, law or no law, courts or no
courts—as long as criminal assaults on innocent women continue,
lynch law will prevail, and bl[ood] will be shed."

Why dwell on all this now? America got along just fine for
decades without having to face up to these pogroms of the 1920s.

What is the point of excavating such ugliness years after the fact? Why not let it all fade into blissful ignorance as we all start with a clean fresh slate?

Michael Hausfeld's answer: "Before you start fresh, you have to clean up the debts of the past."

Hausfeld's career as a would-be righter of historic wrongs did not begin with the Tulsa case, or even with the Swiss banking cases—in which he was one of the lead attorneys—but more than two decades ago, with a civil case, against Andrija Artukovic, the most notorious war criminal from Yugoslavia.

Artukovic, former minister of internal affairs in the Nazi-controlled Croatia, was in charge of the police and paramilitary units that murdered and tortured tens of thousands of Jews and other so-called undesirables. These agents of Nazism thought nothing of burying people alive or beating them to death with sledgehammers. Artukovic fled after the war, taking a circuitous route through Europe, with a year-long stop in a Catholic monastery in Ireland, before washing up with a false name in Southern California.

He was ordered deported in 1952 for having overstayed his visa, but, citing fear of persecution, he convinced a judge to let him stay. He was still in California more than two decades later when Hausfeld went after him for damages on behalf of Holocaust survivors for "deprivations of life and property suffered by Jews in Yugoslavia during World War II." The judge dismissed the complaint in January 1985 on several grounds, noting, among other reasons, that the statute of limitations for his civil damages had passed, that international law did not apply in this case, and that though Artukovic's actions violated the "laws of humanity," they did not violate the laws of war.

The judge apparently also had another concern, as Hausfeld recalls. "If I grant the relief you request," he remembers the judge asking, "what will keep blacks from suing plantation owners for slavery in the United States?"

The next year, Artukovic's long sojourn in the United States finally came to an end. He was deported to Yugoslavia to stand trial for war crimes. In rejecting his appeal to avoid extradition, the U.S. District Court for the Central District of California noted his complicity in numerous crimes, including the murder of the entire civilian population of several villages by machine-gun fire in early 1942 and the crushing, under moving tanks, of several hundred persons machine-gunned in another region the following year. In Yugolsavia, Artukovic, at that point in failing health, was sentenced to death by firing squad but died in a prison hospital before the sentence could be carried out.

Although he lost the court battle with Artukovic, for Hausfeld the case was something of a milestone. He had gone to court many times before to raise social justice issues—on behalf of women and African Americans, in particular. But by the time the Artukovic case came around, he had a deeper understanding of the law, a more developed philosophical framework, and a better sense of how to take the battle onto unexplored turf. He sees a direct line from that case to the Holocaust cases and the Tulsa complaint.

That line extends to a suit against Barclays Bank, British Petroleum, Exxon, and a host of other companies that did business with South Africa's apartheid regime. That suit seeks compensation, a measure of "rough justice," for members of Khulumani, the victims' group in South Africa, who suffered grievously under the apartheid regime. It, in effect, seeks to make foreign corporations answerable for apartheid itself—for the pass laws, the poor housing, the daily humiliations; for the torture, the murders, the unspeakable atrocities.

"Defendants' conduct was so integrally connected to the abuses that apartheid would not have occurred in the same way without their participation," argues the complaint. The essence, as summed up by Hausfeld, is that "companies should be responsible for what they do." If companies aided and abetted apartheid, fully aware of the abuses that regime committed, they must be held accountable.

South African President Thabo Mbeki has criticized the suits: "We consider it completely unacceptable that matters that are central to the future of our country should be adjudicated in foreign courts which bear no responsibility for the well-being of our country or the promotion of national reconciliation," said Mbeki.

Hausfeld thought the concern was misplaced. The groups and lawyers involved, he said, are working out "an exit strategy which would increase investment in South Africa and strengthen the economy.... We're not bomb throwers."

The lawsuit, in other words, was not just about the law. It was ultimately about politics—as indeed all of these cases essentially are, as Stuart Eizenstat well understood. Looking back on the Holocaust assets negotiations, Eizenstat observed, "The lawsuits were simply a vehicle for a titanic political struggle."

As if to underscore the point, South Africa's justice minister, Penuell Maduna, revealed in a June 2003 interview with Johannesburg's *Sunday Independent* that South Africa was trying to work out a deal whereby the big corporations would *voluntarily* pay some form of reparations and thereby avoid the American lawsuits: "Business has been talking to us with their lawyers. They said they are willing to work with us to convince American courts that as South Africans we can find workable and less destructive solutions." Accusing the American lawyers of "victim abuse," Maduna added: "You may have all sorts of legitimate reasons to run to an American court, but it may turn out not to be the best thing to do if it were to put our economy through serious turbulence."

Hausfeld, of course, disagrees. And the exit strategy he has in mind is not the same as the one Mbeki has endorsed. The people around the negotiating table, Hausfeld believes, should represent not just the government and big business. There also has to be a chair for the group of social institutions that constitute "civil society." And there must certainly be a chair for victims—just as there was with the Holocaust cases.

The issue of governmental reparations was no less politically charged within South Africa—which is partly why only in 2003, some eight years after passage of the act creating the Truth and Reconciliation Commission, that government finally settled the question of reparations for those who had testified before the TRC. *Why should we have to pay for the sins of an earlier government?* some members of the ruling African National Congress had asked. Others had suggested that, in seeking money, the victims were somehow being crass. *The fight for liberation was not about money,* they pointed out; *it was about freedom. Weren't we all victims?* went another argument. *Why should these chosen victims get something that we all won't get?*

In the end, President Mbeki signed off on an award of 30,000 rands (or about $4,000) apiece for the roughly 22,000 victims who had come forward to tell their stories. "Combined with community reparations and assistance through opportunities and services, we hope these disbursements will help acknowledge the suffering these individuals experienced, and offer some relief," said Mbeki. It was much less than the TRC had recommended and much less than the victims had been led to expect. Indeed, it was because so many felt abandoned by the government and frustrated by its lack of charity that they had turned to the American courts in the first place—and, in doing so, had gotten the attention of politicians who had underestimated the potency of their political appeal.

If success in winning reparations for historical wrongs is largely about politics, then what about the efforts of Americans to get reparations for slavery and its aftermath?

The basic argument is clear as rainwater: *Slavery was a crime as horrible as any imaginable. People were tortured, enslaved, and unfairly deprived of the fruits of their labor. They were denied the right to hand down any appreciable assets. And their descendants, who were promised freedom and forty acres, were lynched, segregated, discriminated against, and in virtually every way excluded from enjoying the full fruits of freedom. They never got their land. And they only recently have been given the opportunity to earn anything approximating fair compensation. Hence a debt is owed.*

It is the argument that Martin Lurther King Jr. made in a *Playboy* magazine interview in 1965: "Can any fair-minded citizen deny that the Negro has been deprived? Few people reflect that for two centuries the Negro was enslaved, and robbed of any wages—potential accrued wealth which would have been the legacy of his descendants. *All* of America's wealth today could not adequately compensate its Negroes for his centuries of exploitation and humiliation."

Some are now saying that time has finally arrived to begin paying off that debt. Raymond A. Winbush, director of the Institute for Urban Research at Morgan State University, notes that this is not the first era in which the demand has been made. It was made shortly after the Civil War, and with the dawn of Marcus Garvey's brand of Black Nationalism, in the early part of the twentieth century.

"Why is it that Japanese Americans received an apology and compensatory measures . . . but Black Americans in all but a few instances have been unsuccessful in their efforts for remedies to the crimes inflicted upon them? Why do Jews continue to litigate successfully for and receive billions of dollars from nations and corporations nearly sixty years after the Holocaust . . . yet African Americans are subjected to paternalistic rejections of their movement for reparations for 350 years of enslavement and domestic apartheid? I believe it is because the history of Black/white relations in this country is so long and sordid that reparations for damages done . . . would call for an enormous upheaval of the social fabric of the United States unmatched even by *Brown v. Board,*" writes Winbush in *Should America Pay?*

Every year since 1989, Congressman John Conyers has introduced legislation asking, so far without success, for creation of a commission to study the question of reparations for African Americans. The commission, similar in concept to the body that recommended redress for Japanese Americans interned during World War II, would be charged with documenting the lingering impact of the institution that Conyers believes continues to wreak havoc on black life.

In *Black Wealth/White Wealth* social scientist Melvin L. Oliver and Thomas M. Shapiro provide a glimpse of what such an exhaustive study might show. After reviewing reams of historical and economic data, they conclude that whites, at every income level, possess several times more wealth than blacks. They believe that the majority of the difference—perhaps three-quarters of it—can be explained by America's history of discrimination and "racialized" policies, beginning with the slave trade: "Slaves were by law not able to own property or accumulate assets. In contrast, no matter how poor whites were, they had the right—if they were males, that is . . . to buy land, enter into contracts, own businesses, and develop wealth assets that could build equity and economic self-sufficiency for themselves and their families." Blacks, who could not accumulate such riches, also "confronted a world that systematically thwarted any attempts to economically better their lives." This "inheritance of accumulated disadvantages over generations," argue the authors, continues to undermine the economic well-being of African Americans. They see a strong (though not politically plausible) case for reparations for black Americans.

Burt Neuborn, a New York University law professor who worked on the Holocaust banking cases, thinks the litigation against the Swiss banks may provide a model for descendants of slaves. "The critical question," he argued in the 2003 edition of the *New York University Annual Survey of American Law*, "is whether litigation seeking restitution of the unjust enrichment flowing from slavery can replicate the three crucial components of the Holocaust litigation: (1) the identification of massive wealth transfers to identifiable recipients that unjustly enriched the recipients; (2) a demonstration that the wealth transfers were unlawful; and

(3) the ability to reverse the transfers by requiring restitution of unjustly acquired profits to identifiable victims."

It is easy to prove, he points out, that wealth was unjustly transferred. And it's even possible to make a case—under international law, perhaps—that the wealth transfers were illegal. The difficulty, as he sees it, is "the linking of identifiable victims with identifiable unjustly enriched beneficiaries." One way to get around that, he says, is to point out that at the time when America should have put things right—at the time the slaves were freed—it did not choose to do so: "and since the passage of time renders it impossible to re-capture that moment, the only just approach is to adopt political programs designed to cope with the lingering consequences of such a massive unjust enrichment of white America."

That is the approach Randall Robinson essentially endorsed in *The Debt,* in which he argued for the creation of a government-funded trust that would support economic empowerment, civil rights advocacy, and education—with special efforts directed toward those black children most at risk. Just debating the proposal, suggested Robinson, would be good for America: "The catharsis occasioned by a full-scale reparations debate could . . . launch us with a critical mass into a surge of black self-discovery. . . . We could disinter a buried history, connect it to another, more recent and mistold, and give it as a healing to the whole of our people, to the whole of America."

Whether such a debate really would be "healing" is very much an open question; but it is telling that Conyers—who consistently points out that his bill would not provide reparations but only a study of the issue—can never get his bill out of committee. Year after year, he puts the proposal forth; and year after year, it dies. The very subject turns so many people off, or makes them so uncomfortable, that they would rather not even have a serious conversation about it.

Many advocates saw the United Nations World Conference

Against Racism as the perfect opportunity to jump-start that extended conversation. Prior to the conference itself—held in Durban, South Africa, August 31 through September 7, 2001—a series of preparatory meetings (PrepComs, in UN parlance) were held in various cities around the world. Some of the leading lights of the reparations movement and even representatives of "mainstream" civil rights organizations faithfully attended many of those meetings. In corridors, meeting rooms, and hotel lobbies they made the case to delegates and others from around the world that slavery and the slave trade were crimes against humanity and that reparations had to be addressed. At one point a UN subcommission adopted a resolution on "recognition of responsibility and reparation for massive and flagrant violations of human rights which constituted crimes against humanity and took place during slavery and the colonial period."

The delegates from the United States never bought it. Indeed, they threatened to walk out of the convention if such language was taken seriously. In fact, the U.S. delegation did withdraw—not over reparations, but over anti-Israeli and anti-Semitic language that certain documents contained; but they left no doubt that as far as they were concerned a debate on reparations was about as welcome as a visit from Fidel Castro. Even Congressman Tom Lantos, who said he had "zero hang-ups" with the word *reparations,* pleaded with the advocates to use another phrase. In the pragmatic interest of winning support, he argued, they should rally around remedies that were not race based, that would not polarize Congress and endanger political support.

That it took some sixty years before Oklahoma and Florida could even acknowledge that pogroms had occurred in their states, that the episodes were denied a place in history books, that most Americans to this day have no idea that such things occurred, says something profound about how difficult it is to own up to racial sins. For many, it's easier to pretend they never happened. And yet for the same reason that thoughtful people reject Holocaust denial, many blacks reject that form of denial; for it is a way of saying that the losses and the suffering of our ancestors don't matter, which is uncomfortably close to saying that we don't matter.

For those whose links to a painful past are too immediate to forget, such denial can be a form of emotional abuse—a point made to me by several survivors of a spectacularly shameful episode in Virginia's history.

Farmville is a small town little more than an hour's drive from the state capital of Richmond; and it came to symbolize, in some respects, Virginia's and the South's resistance to integration. In 1954, when the U.S. Supreme Court decided the era of "separate but equal" was over and ordered schools desegregated, Virginia's elite essentially declared "No way!" Under the banner of "massive resistance," the legislature took one radical step after another in an attempt to cling to segregation as a way of life. Among other extraordinary—not to mention unconstitutional—acts, the legislature prohibited expenditure of funds on integrated schools and funneled public money to so-called segregation academies that sprung up around the state.

Prince Edward County, where Farmville is located, eventually ended public education altogether. From 1959 through much of 1964 (when the Supreme Court ordered the schools reopened), all public schools were shuttered. If you were white, that was not a tragedy. County officials provided what amounted to vouchers and other financial support to white students, who went to the purportedly private segregation academies. Black students were not so lucky. Most saw their educational hopes simply wither.

The lucky ones managed to go to school elsewhere. Vonita Foster was preparing to enter the fourth grade when the schools were shut down. Her parents, who owned a local cleaners, sent her to stay with relatives in Baltimore, where she was able to continue her education. When she returned to Virginia two years later, her father rented a house in a nearby county. No family

member ever lived there. Instead, her father would drive Vonita
to the empty house every morning so she could be picked up for
transport to her segregated school.

Few of her friends were so well off. Most languished in
Farmville. When the schools finally opened, the students were so
far behind that college seemed an unattainable dream. "They did
not think they could do the work," recalled Foster. "I think that
we lost a lot of the doctors we would have had, a lot of teachers
who could have helped," she told me when we talked following
my visit to Farmville.

Several people in Farmville made the same point. Armstead
Reid, a postman and a Farmville town councilman, was eight
when the schools closed. During most of the period of the closure,
he received virtually no education. Reid managed to finish high
school once the schools reopened, but he never really made up for
the lost years. When his musical talent resulted in an invitation to
attend college, he passed up the opportunity. "I was scared," he
told me over lunch. "I didn't think I could do it."

The extent of the harm, as Foster sees it, is incalculable. And
she resents the fact that, for so long, the damage went essentially
unacknowledged, that people apparently were so eager to bury
that era and its survivors "under the sand."

In recent years, thanks in part to Foster and Viola Baskerville,
a black state legislator raised not far from Farmville, that has
begun to change. Under Foster's prodding, Baskerville took on
the cause of the hundreds of blacks denied an education in
Farmville. Originally, Baskerville thought she might be able to get
an apology out of the state, but found many of her colleagues
reluctant to take that step. Instead, she settled for a bill, passed in
2003, that expressed "profound regret over the 1959–1964 closing
of the public schools." The measure also acknowledged that
because of the closure "more than 2,300 African-American children . . . with only a few exceptions, remained unschooled for at
least four of these five years."

In 2003, after passage of Baskerville's bill, local school administrators sponsored a ceremony during which they awarded honorary high school diplomas to some four hundred current and former Farmville residents who had been denied an education. The event was so successful, emotionally resonant, and well-attended that a similar ceremony was planned for 2004. Foster was also working on a dinner, tentatively themed "Lest we forget," to commemorate those abandoned students.

Meanwhile, Baskerville was girding for the next battle. She was seeking scholarships for those Virginia residents, and their descendants, adversely affected by the closing of the schools. She was seeking, in other words, a modest form of reparation, nothing more than that won by those victims of the Nazi Holocaust in Austria who could apply to the "General Settlement Fund for Victims of National Socialism" for compensation for uncompleted or interrupted education. Baskerville was hopeful that the attention generated in 2004 by the fiftieth anniversary of the Supreme Court desegregation decision might shame her reluctant colleagues into voting for the scholarship bill. But she was far from sanguine. For there were many Virginians all too eager to wash their hands of any responsibility for those unfortunate blacks; many Virginians all too eager to forget that there was a time, not long ago, when their widely revered leaders were so profoundly racist that they were willing to destroy the future of an entire generation of black children—many of whom, despite the unrelenting assault on their well-being, managed to survive into the present day, albeit irremediably scarred by the experience.

But even without the explosive element of race, reparations is a difficult subject. No country, no people, no regime willingly accepts the blame for having done horrible things, along with the responsibility for trying to repair damaged lives and replace confiscated or stolen goods. And once race enters the room, what was already a difficult conversation becomes virtually impossible. While one side wants to talk about how to settle a debt, the other is denying that any debt is due: *I didn't own slaves, why should I pay? My ancestors weren't even in this country when your people were enslaved. Wouldn't you have been worse off without slavery? At least you are now a citizen of the United States. Yes, some bad things happened, but that was long, long ago: Can't you just get over it?*

"To correct a historical wrong—be it for slavery, or segregation, for discrimination or exclusion—is to drive a wedge even more deeply between angry blacks who demand compensation for their losses and indignant whites who disavow any responsibility. The Tulsa race riot lasted less than sixteen hours, but its search for closure overlapped America's own struggle to make peace with a painful past," wrote James Hirsch in *Riot and Rememberance*.

In some things, it seems, there is something of a historical statute of limitations. Shakespeare apparently had it backward. What he no doubt should have written was: "The good that men do lives after them; the evil is interred with their bones." So the same son of the South who clings so tightly to his Confederate flag, who argues for its continued relevance, dismisses slavery as insignificant in terms of modern problems. The same patriot who believes heroic acts of World War I and World War II are worthy of celebration does not believe shameful acts from those same eras are worthy of condemnation. There are people who arrived in America less than a decade ago who—through their payment of taxes, through their participation in the American political process—assume responsibility for myriad things they personally had nothing to do with. They pay off debts incurred by past presidents; accept treaty obligations negotiated by long-departed diplomats; but they also, for the most part, accept an argument that says, in effect, "Racial wrongs, and any responsibility to atone for them, do not persist beyond a generation."

Why do so many of us live in such segregated communities? Why did the O. J. Simpson case cast such a polarizing shadow? Why are the statistics of socioeconomic well-being so divergent for people of different hues? Part of the answer lies in history: in decisions sanctioned and carried out by the state that elevated one set of people above another.

The plea for American reparations is, as much as anything, a plea to learn or to reconsider that history—and to reconsider, as well, the assumption that the way the world is—with one racial group significantly better off than another—is simply the natural state of things. In *Paying for the Past,* Christian Pross observes, "The reparations program set the stage for a change in consciousness and for a transformation . . . in the way German society dealt with the Nazi past." The hope of many of those in America who support reparations is that the educational process that accompanies the debate will spark a similar transformation.

Tim Madigan holds himself out as an example of how immersion in previously forbidden history can deeply change perceptions. The research he did for *The Burning* was "a life-changing odyssey. Early in the process, I began to suspect that a crucial piece remained missing from America's long attempts at racial reconciliation. Too many in this country remained as ignorant as I was. Too many were just as oblivious to some of the darkest moments in our history, a legacy of which Tulsa is both a tragic example and a shameful metaphor. How can we heal when we don't know what we're healing from?"

In an essay included in *Paying for the Past,* Erich Loewy makes a point about the importance of acknowledgment: "When those responsible for causing the damage (or those historically associated with causing it) are themselves willing to apply balm to the wounds they caused, healing will proceed more easily." He goes on to condemn the Germans, whose acceptance of reparations was "forced and grudging," for missing the opportunity to embrace a less acrimonious process.

When it comes to the issue of reparations, of course, the United States is not even remotely in the position of Germany following World War II. No one has defeated the United States. No one accuses the current generation of U.S. leaders of supporting slavery—or implementing Jim Crow. And no one is in the powerful position of the Allies demanding that historical wrongs be set right.

Nor is there the equivalent of the Treaty of Waitangi, a historical document that has the force of law that can point the way to a reallocation of resources. There *is* General William T. Sherman's Special Field Order Number 15: the 1865 document that promised up to forty acres to former slaves; it didn't really say anything about a mule. And there is a growing clamor on the part of those who say it is time that Sherman's commitment be kept—and who suggest that lawsuits, or a reinterpretation of the law, may be the way to make it happen.

Certainly, as Burt Neuborn and others have made clear, powerful legal arguments can be made on behalf of reparations for African Americans—arguments that, as Hausfeld observes, follow logically from those that worked so well in the Holocaust cases. Those cases also dealt with very old claims and with losses that, in many instances, were difficult to precisely calculate. But in the end even Hausfeld acknowledges that such a case—a general case for reparations for African Americans—cannot be won on legal grounds.

For one thing, there is the problem of time. Not merely decades but centuries have elapsed since slavery was introduced. Also, there are virtually no descendants with identifiable, quantifiable property claims, partly because slaves were considered property themselves and, of course, were barred, for the most part, from acquiring other substantial assets. One can certainly make the argument, logically and persuasively, that "what I am now is diminished by what occurred three hundred years ago," notes Hausfeld. But that is not the same as proving it in a court of law.

Yet it's impossible not to take Eizenstat's point that, in the end, the law is not what moves societies to change. At the most, it gets an issue on the bargaining table. For law, in its essence, is nothing more than a codification of the rules societies agree to obey—

subject to change at society's whim when a new consensus or circumstance compels it.

The law did not protect the residents of Greenwood or Rosewood because the law is the handmaiden of a particular society; and since the America of the 1920s was not interested in protecting black folks or their supposed rights, the "reign of terror against African Americans," to use the language of the Rosewood report, was allowed to proceed unchecked.

Put another way, it was not law that made the Treaty of Waitangi so potent, but the evolution of New Zealand's society. No treaty suddenly becomes valid some 135 years after it was signed. Instead, New Zealand's leaders recognized that a festering wrong was eating away the core of their society and that it somehow had to be dealt with. By the same token, Swiss and German bankers didn't wake up one fine morning and say, "Hmmm . . . after fifty-some years, we now have an obligation to give those poor Jews their money back." They responded simply because conditions were created that made it uncomfortable for them to continue to ignore the voices of those demanding that a wrong be righted.

Will America reach that point when it comes to the issue of slavery? Obviously not anytime soon. At a Harvard University conference in September 2003, Michael Dawson, a government professor and polling expert, reported on a survey that attempted to gauge public support for the idea of making amends for slavery. Only 30 percent of whites—compared to 79 percent of blacks—felt blacks were due an apology for slavery. Even fewer felt blacks deserved money. Four percent of whites—compared to 67 percent of blacks—were in favor of compensation to the descendants of slaves. "The racial differences . . . are as large as any I have seen," said Dawson.

Still, the issue refuses to go away. I received one indication of how insistent and—in a sense, mainstream—the question of reparations has become when I dropped by the office of hip-hop mogul

Russell Simmons and noticed that his *One World* magazine carried an ad for Phat Farm footwear with copy that screamed:

> *Reparations is* not *a racial issue.*
> *It's an America justice issue.*

Reparations is also not an issue, to use Mahara Okeroa's phrase, that is just about "a package of money and a package of apologies." It is about competing views of history and competing visions of the future—and about radically different perspectives on the continuing significance of the sins of the Founding Fathers. It is about the need of people not unlike those who have appeared before truth commissions around the world to see to it that their particular truth is heard.

It remains unclear to what extent America is capable of hearing truths so at odds with cherished perceptions of the American past and with such far-ranging implications for the American present. The paradox is that by the time we arrive at a point where most Americans are willing to listen without prejudice, the debate over reparations will be largely moot; for we likely also will have arrived at a point where America no longer flinches from responsibility for making all of its citizens whole.

The argument for reparations is essentially an argument about keeping promises and restoring a damaged community, about giving people restitution for what was taken, about providing opportunities that were denied. The problem is not that black Americans never got forty acres (and a mule); it is that so much was taken and so little given that impoverishment and despair became self-perpetuating. To correct that, one need not arrive at a figure of precisely what was taken, or calculate the present value of forty acres and write a check. One need not, in fact, talk about reparations at all. One need only make a decision that a damaged community, whatever the cost, must be restored.

Congressman Lantos has a point. It is possible to provide a community with jobs, with better schooling, with economic development without labeling it payment of a debt for the sins of the Fathers. And, indeed, if we ever reach the point when America is prepared to do that, there will be no reason to talk reparations. Instead we will simply be asking: What must we do to provide all Americans with the wherewithal to achieve whatever it is they deserve?

6.

MEMORY AND TRUTH

FOR PERFORMANCE ARTIST AND PLAYWRIGHT Claudia Stevens, memory is life. Or it might be more accurate to say that memory is art. But it is more than that; it is also rebirth. For, in both a professional and personal sense, recovered memories were the instrument of her re-creation.

Stevens is slender, dark-haired, and poised; and her words come out not so much leisurely as carefully, in a soft voice and with the precise delivery of a person accustomed to being onstage. She was raised in a rural area of Northern California where her parents, who had come to America from England, had a farm and taught in one-room schools in the nearby hills. Conditions in the schools, which Stevens briefly attended, were a bit primitive; water was brought in daily in their pickup truck. But rural California seemed to be an ideal place for a family eager to escape the tensions of urban life.

Her parents, she would later discover, were escaping something infinitely more traumatic than the hurly-burly of London or New York. That discovery came when she was nineteen, just after her sophomore year at Vassar. She had gone to college with the idea of perhaps becoming a doctor. But she was also a talented musician, a pianist and operatic singer, with tentative thoughts of a career in the arts. So she was excited when she was accepted into an elite group of young pianists for summer study with the famed Leon Fleisher at the Music Academy of the West in Santa Barbara.

It was the summer of 1968. America was in turmoil over the Vietnam War, Martin Luther King Jr. had been assassinated, and Bobby Kennedy would soon die as well. But Stevens was less focused on politics than on the academy and on the validation it had given her as a musician.

Her sister was studying nearby, at Stanford; and one evening they took advantage of their proximity to meet in Palo Alto. Over dinner—the main dish, as Stevens recalls, was a pork roast—her sister turned to her and said, "Do you know we are Jews?"

The news hit with all the effect of a lightning bolt. She stammered out a response: "What? How can that be?"

Her sister, a student nurse, explained that she had learned the news recently from a patient who knew their grandmother— really their stepgrandmother. Granny, who had lived with them briefly when they were children, was now in a nursing home in San Francisco. Why not pay her a visit?

Stevens took the bus to San Francisco and found the place—a Jewish nursing home on Silver Avenue; and upon entering Granny's room, she noticed a photograph of her grandfather. She remembered the picture from childhood but saw it in a way she had never seen it before: "He had a Jewish face. . . . This was the photograph of a Jewish man." Nonetheless, she asked the question: "Are we Jews?"

Her grandmother, who had been asked by Stevens's father to keep the secret, was unable to lie.

At the time, Stevens was more than a little off balance. Her mood was "mostly wonderment. It was an unusual environment, a nursing home, and I was seeing her after all this time. . . . She felt very awkward about talking about the past."

A few days later her father, who had learned of the visit to Granny, showed up in Santa Barbara, carrying photographs and documents. As they sat under an umbrella at the beach, he spread the materials out on a table and told her about his and her mother's past. She learned that although her parents had lived in England, they were not British. Her mother hailed from Austria and her father from what is now part of the Czech Republic. During that conversation, and during subsequent talks, she also learned a great deal about a history that had been hidden as the couple cobbled together a life—ostensibly non-Jewish—in America.

Her father had fled from Czechoslovakia as the horrors of the Holocaust became plain: "He had come on an illegal transport, a ship that was prevented from landing in British Palestine because the doors there were already closed to immigration. The ship had to linger at sea for months under terrible conditions—starvation, disease—with no medical supplies, barely any coal. They were just drifting, waiting for a chance to land. Then they rescued seven hundred and fifty Polish Jews from another sinking freighter and landed everyone somehow at night, during a storm when the British weren't looking. The commander of this transport saved fifteen hundred Jews and he's an unknown person."

The story of her grandmother's attempt to follow her son was even more poignant: "My father's mother was still in Czechoslovakia in the fall of 1940. The Jewish community there was completely desperate to get out as the Nazis closed in. Her group of nearly four thousand refugees went down the Danube by riverboat. When they got to the Black Sea, they boarded three small freighters. And these ships had similar experiences—no food, disease, no fuel. After several months at sea—and you can imagine, from the Black Sea to the coast of Israel isn't very far; it would be like a day's journey today. But it took months for these people.

"Finally the three ships came into the harbor at Haifa, one after the other. But the British would not allow them to land. Everyone was to be deported, put onto an ocean liner that happened to be available. As many as possible were squeezed onto this large ship—the *Patria*. Hundreds of mattresses were brought on board, and the deck was covered with provisions for sending the refugees to Mauritius, which was then a British prison island in the Indian Ocean. . . . Then the refugee leadership on the *Patria*, together with members of the Jewish leadership on shore, devised a plan to disable the ship by blowing a hole in the side. Dynamite was smuggled on board secretly, and the passengers were told to gather on the upper deck on the morning of the deportation.

"There was a huge explosion that morning, ripping a large gash in the *Patria*. Instead of just being disabled, it listed and began to sink rapidly. The hole was so large the sea rushed in and drowned nearly everybody still below deck. And the people above—I'm sure my grandmother was above—many of them jumped overboard because they were so close they could see the beach there . . . the Promised Land, as it were. And I think she jumped, tried to swim. At least her friend who survived said that she had. She was either struck by falling cargo, which is how many of them were killed, or drowned. . . . All those mattresses that had been on the deck slid off into the sea and covered it, like a sheet of ice, and people were trapped underneath."

Once Stevens recovered from the shock of the revelations, things began to fall into place. "Spiritually, I think I had already rejected traditional Christianity." Yet she still felt a sense of emptiness. Suddenly belonging to a people "with two thousand years of suffering behind them" provided a powerful sense of connection. It also made her feel freer to think about a life in the arts: "Much of the musical world then was Jewish, in the way much of it is Asian now." No longer would she be, in their eyes, "a little goy, a wanna-be musician with no soul." But she sensed something more profound about this revelation. "I had been a Christian. I had experienced the world as a Christian does. Yet there was an underlay of something else that was unspoken."

Things came back to her: an electricity in the air when Jews had been mentioned or Israel was in the news, her father's deep depression during Christmas. She later found out he had secretly observed Jewish High Holidays all those years. And there was something her mother had told her as a child to encourage her piano study that now made perfect sense. Practice, she had told her. "It might save your life someday." Stevens now knew that to be a reference to those who had avoided the gas chamber by performing in the concentration camps. "How could I not have realized?" she wondered.

Yet she felt no anger at having been deceived. She knew her parents were only trying to protect her; to shelter her from anti-Semitism, to give her a clean slate, so to speak. What she felt instead was happiness—for she now had answers—and also a sense of freedom.

"A lot of things made sense and there was a sudden new opportunity to have a truly interesting life. I realized that there were going to be ramifications. . . . It wasn't just a story of one's relatives. It got to the whole nature of what it means to be. . . . I think I had been afraid of being on too simple and clear a path, and I realized then I didn't have to be on it anymore."

Stevens completed her music studies at Vassar and earned a doctorate in piano from Boston University. She embarked on a successful career performing contemporary classical music. Important composers were writing pieces for her, and she had a record deal. But in her thirties, she began to feel a need for change. "I didn't really love this music enough." She had also come into contact with "total performance"—whereby one could play and sing, do movement or recitation—taking theater in unexpected and powerful directions. Other pianists could do more or less what she had been doing, she reasoned; but in this new art form she could perhaps create something uniquely her own.

For inspiration, she turned to her past, and to the pasts of those who had brought her into the world. She crafted a piece called

Playing Paradis, in which she assumes the persona of a blind musical prodigy in eighteenth-century Vienna. The performance deals with the subject, as Stevens put it, "of being a deceived child—but also with the trade-off between happy ignorance and deep expression." Other works dealt directly with the Holocaust. In *A Table Before Me* she used documents obtained from Austrian State Archives in her mother's unsuccessful efforts to redeem a life insurance policy confiscated by the Nazis during World War II. In *An Evening with Madame F* she played the role that her mother, in a sense, envisioned: a pianist and singer whose talents keep her alive in a Nazi concentration camp.

"What I am doing has less to do with 'never forget,'" said Stevens, "and more with how to use experience for artistic purposes." Yet her audiences—if the one I saw in New York is typical—do indeed see her performance as a way of reminding the world that such things should never happen again. They see her as something of a channel to (or a channeler of) the past. For every inquiry about art, there are two about the political, historical, and emotional meanings surrounding the Holocaust and the work—a body of work that is, in large measure, about memory and the implications of remembering, and that derives its power not merely from one woman's metamorphosis, but also from the connection of her journey of self-discovery to an infinitely larger quest for meaning in a history that defies comprehension.

To what extent do we have a collective responsibility to remember? And having remembered, how do we proceed? Art cannot definitively answer those questions. Neither, in fact, can politics. But increasingly, those are the kinds of questions that are ending up in the public, legal, and political arenas.

In the last decade and a half we have seen the flowering of a new movement: a movement for recovered memory. I'm not talking about individuals who supposedly suddenly recover, in intricate detail, memories of a childhood trauma previously repressed. Nor am I talking about people—though there are powerful parallels—

recovering personal links to the Holocaust. I'm talking about something with considerably broader ramifications: the recovery not of
personal memory but of historical memory. There is a new resolve
on the part of many—individuals and nations alike—to excavate
painful parts of the past. It is fueled not by nostalgia, but by a sense
that the future is hostage, in some respects, to the past and to history's outstanding debts—a sense that moving forward requires, as
former Greensboro mayor Carolyn Allen put it, getting the "bumps
out of your history."

That impulse, that need, to set right what was wrong is a large
part of what fueled renewal of interest in places like Rosewood
and Greenwood decades after the atrocities occurred and official
memories were buried in a vault of denial. It is what drove people
toward yet another reckoning for the sins of the Holocaust. It is
what impels a reexamination of Farmville. It is what has pro-
pelled troubled societies, from Peru to East Timor, from South
Africa to Sri Lanka to Sierra Leone, to ask—as they put together
truth commissions—whether the key to reconciliation is buried
somewhere in the past; whether, if they can come to terms with
their history, they can happily embrace a new day.

"Because they [truth commissions] do respond to such an
apparently fundamental and widely felt need—first and foremost,
to know and acknowledge the truth, to "unsilence" a long-denied
past—it is likely we will only see more of them," commented
Priscilla Hayner in *Unspeakable Truths*. When I checked in with
Hayner in August 2003, her prediction was very much in the
process of becoming fact. She noted that twenty-five or so truth
commissions so far had been born and that several others were in
various stages of formation.

In *The Guilt of Nations,* historian Elazar Barkan observed,
"This desire to redress the past is a growing trend, which touches
our life at multiple levels, and it is central to our moral self-
understanding as individuals and members of groups the world
over. In a post–Cold War world we tend to pay increased atten-

tion to moral responsibility. . . . No longer does the brute and immediate existential security need of the country form the sole legitimate justification or motive in formulating a foreign policy. Instead opposition to genocide, support for human rights, and the fear of being implicated in crimes against humanity (even by inaction) have become practical, not merely lofty, ideals. These ideals increasingly shape political decisions and the international scene."

Amnesia is not an option, we increasingly are told. Because healing requires forgiveness, and forgiveness first requires remembering. As East Timor truth commissioner Isabel Amaral-Gueterres put it: "For some people, it may seem better to leave the past untouched. But the past does not go away and, if untreated, may eat away at those people and maybe even destroy them. Remembering is not easy, but forgetting may be impossible."

At the first formal meeting of South Africa's TRC, in December 1995, Chairman and Archbishop Desmond Tutu lectured his fellow commissioners: "They say that those who suffer from amnesia, those who forget the past, are doomed to repeat it. It is not dealing with the past to say facilely, 'Let bygones be bygones.' For then they won't be bygones. Our country, our society would be doomed to the instability of uncertainty—the uncertainty engendered by not knowing when yet another scandal of the past would hit the headlines, when another skeleton would be dragged out of the cupboard. We will be engaging in what should be a corporate nationwide process of healing through contrition, confession, and forgiveness. To be able to forgive one needs to know whom one is forgiving and why. That is why the truth is so central to this whole exercise."

That observation was echoed by Rosalina Tuyuc, founder of the National Association of Guatemalan Widows. "Forgiving doesn't mean forgetting. First we need to know who to forgive. . . . And if we don't manage to establish who was responsible, history may repeat itself," she said in an interview published in *The Unesco Courier*.

In *The Book of Laughter and Forgetting* Milan Kundera famously declared, "The struggle of man against power is the struggle of memory against forgetting." And, more and more, people are taking those words to heart as they raise their voices and solemnly swear, "We will never forget!"

But as with all things of importance in life, the reality of remembering is complicated. It does not always work the way we like to believe it does. It certainly does not always follow what might be called the three truth commission commandments:

1. The truth can be discovered.
2. The truth can be agreed to.
3. The truth will, in some sense, set us free—free to reconcile with one another, free to imbibe the wisdom of experience so that never again will others have to endure what we went through.

Discovering the truth:

As victims from Argentina to Rwanda have discovered, truth can be an extremely elusive thing. The craving to know is rarely satisfied, since the answers are almost always incomplete.

Some years ago, Dumisa Ntsebeza, a South African TRC commissioner and chief of its investigative unit, shared some of his frustrations during dinner in a Cape Town restaurant. "I ask myself," he said at one point, "is it expected of me to really investigate thirty-four years of South African history?" He went on to catalog the obstacles, beginning with the fact that the TRC had not exactly gotten off to a running start. At the first formal TRC meeting, the one where Tutu waxed eloquent about the TRC's mission and its search for truth, Ntsebeza was wondering how thorough that search could be. "We didn't have an office. We didn't know where we were going to operate from. . . . *Nobody knew.*" And once things got up and running, there was never enough time or resources to investigate everything.

How large of an investigative force would he have needed to

really get the job done? "One hundred, two hundred, five hundred," he wondered. Yet he only had sixty investigators, and never all of them at one time. "South Africa is a wide country. We had whole sections of the country [assigned to] only twelve people. I ask myself how was it possible to do the things that we did."

His point, of course, was that despite all his hard work and good intentions, despite all the investigative successes he did have—and there, in fact, were many—there was simply no way to unearth anything approximating the whole truth.

Hugo van der Merwe of the Centre for the Study of Violence and Reconciliation, as noted earlier, made much the same point: "Most victims clearly wanted some kind of truth from the TRC, and not just the truth of their own stories being told and acknowledged as true; they wanted more information, more facts. . . . And I would say that ninety-five percent of the people didn't get that."

South Africa's TRC is the recognized gold standard. Still underresourced as it was, it had so much more than the others, whose search for truth was even more hobbled than Ntsebeza's.

But even had unlimited resources been available, much of the truth would have remained beyond their grasp, if for no other reason than that different people (witnesses, perpetrators, victims) invariably differed on the basic facts. *We didn't beat him to death; he bumped his head. We didn't rape that women; we never saw her. We didn't order that execution; he did it on his own.*

Agreeing on the truth:

Discovering the truth, of course, requires more than just establishing some facts. It also means agreeing on what those facts mean.

In the Greensboro massacre, for instance, many of the facts are no longer in dispute. The protestors assembled, the police vanished, the Klan attacked, and people were killed. What is in dispute is what to make of those facts.

The people behind the truth commission insist that if they can shed new light on what occurred, the city will have to face some harsh truths about itself; that its citizens will be forced to change some cherished assumptions about how enlightened Greensboro actually is and how the city actually functions—and, ultimately, about what it must do if its citizens are to live in harmony.

But that is not necessarily true. Even if people agree that in the Greensboro of 1979 the Ku Klux Klan operated with impunity, and that they were embraced by a significant part of the community, that doesn't mean they believe any of that is relevant to today's Greensboro. All the more so if, as Mayor Keith Holliday insisted, "Half of Greensboro wasn't even alive or living in Greensboro at the time."

Indeed, as far as many are concerned, the 1979 tragedy was a tragic aberration that did all of Greensboro, indeed all of North Carolina, the disservice of making its good citizens look bad. How, if in fact they feel that way, could they see the truth-seeking venture as anything other than a pointless exercise in demagoguery and self-flagellation?

F. W. de Klerk, the former South Africa president who shared the Nobel Peace Prize with Nelson Mandela, was instrumental in bringing the new South Africa into being. But he clearly has a different take on the truth than his counterparts in Mandela's African National Congress. The TRC, in his view, did not so much come up with the truth as with a "version of our past that was fully acceptable to one side only," he told an American audience in 2002.

Allies of former president Jerry Rawlings were just as dismissive of the work of the Ghanaian truth commission—no doubt largely because most of its complaints focused on violations during periods of his rule. The commissioners "clearly show their bias during questioning," complained John Mahama, a member of Parliament and spokesperson for Rawlings's party, the National Democratic Congress. And Rawlings's lawyer, whom I encountered in the office of Ken Attafuah, executive director of Ghana's TRC, seemed to think the proceedings were little more than a joke.

Invariably, truth commissions unearth new and shocking facts. "Many of the revelations have come as a surprise to many of us. There were reports of people killed in shoot-outs; we are now learning there were executions," confided Kweku Etrew Amua-Sekyi, a retired Supreme Court justice and chairman of the Ghanaian commission. But even after those facts are revealed and verified, agreeing on who was ultimately responsible and what needs to change as a consequence are never areas of easy agreement.

The truth will set us free?

Let's speak out to each other by telling the truth, by telling the stories of the past, so that we can walk the road to reconciliation together. That message, so prominently displayed in the Cape Town TRC hearing room, is both compelling and inspiring. Yet as one truth commission after another has realized, reconciliation, however it is defined, requires so much more than crying over the stories of the past. It requires transformation—of individuals and, where countries are concerned, of the very norms of society. Rediscovered history, recovered memories, can no doubt help that process; but they can't force it to take place. By the same token, the idea that documenting atrocities and memorializing the victims will prevent such things from happening anywhere again is rooted much more strongly in faith than in history.

Never again, in other words, is not a plan; it's a prayer. A prayer that we will see the connections from one atrocity to another, that we will see bigoted demagogues exactly for what they are, that we will turn against those who scapegoat others. It is a plea that we remember not just the Holocaust but also how easily it came about.

But there is little reason to believe people typically carry the lessons of one tragedy or one atrocity to another. Even had the world properly documented and mourned the Armenian genocide, there is no reason to believe that doing so would have stopped the Holocaust from happening. Obviously, knowledge of the

Holocaust and memorialization of its victims didn't stop the genocide in Cambodia; and familiarity with the Cambodia genocide didn't prevent the slaughter in Rwanda. "We tried to bear witness, and we did. Apparently the testimony has not been heard," Elie Wiesel told a reporter for the *Chicago Tribune* in 2002.

Political leaders—particularly those who are most belligerent—tend to have limited imaginations. They don't see the genocide that they commit or sanction in the same light as the Holocaust; they don't see the soul of a Jew in a Tutsi or the heart of a Cambodian in a Croat. Each conflict, they convince themselves, is unique. Each targeted group, they tell themselves, is different. Each enemy is uniquely awful or repugnant. So they transfer little moral meaning from one situation to another—not, at least, unless the world rises up in anger and demands a different perspective.

At a public dialogue at New York's Museum of Jewish Heritage, a speaker quite forcefully made the point that if more Nazi war criminals had been prosecuted, Rwanda might never have happened. And I suppose it is possible that we would have seen a lot less genocide in that past sixty years if every known Nazi war criminal had been hunted down and if the message had gone forth that henchmen of criminal regimes elsewhere would be dealt with similarly. But to even suggest the idea is to realize there is no set of conceivable circumstances under which that might have happened. It is also, however, to realize that, in at least some limited sense—with truth commissions sprouting in every corner of the globe, with assorted tribunals around the world prosecuting crimes against humanity, with the birth of an International Criminal Court (that the United States, incidentally, opposed)—we are closer to that ideal than we have ever been. We may at long last be inching closer to something of a consensus on the matter of how to deal with political leaders who do evil things.

We may not be able—or willing—to prevent the next holocaust from happening; but much of the world, at least, has finally come to agree that when lives have been deliberately shattered, especially by the state, someone ought to be responsible for trying to put them back together again—and someone ought to pay a price.

The world, in other words, does change—through absorbing, at least in part, certain lessons of history, even if we must be taught them again and again as new would-be Hitlers appear on the scene, as new victims take their place in line, as the present wipes out much of the memory of the past.

A few years back, something called "black empowerment" was in vogue in business circles in South Africa. It was a plan to allow certain nonwhites, generally those with political influence, to acquire stock under favorable but financially contingent conditions. During that very short era, I met with a South African businesswoman of East Indian descent who had managed to become a significant financial player. She was happy, she said, that South Africa's white corporate establishment had bought into black empowerment, and she certainly recognized that she had benefited from it; but she also realized that any advantage gained by guilt over apartheid was not going to last. White South Africans, she said, were only willing to dwell on apartheid and its evils for so long before they opted to forget it and move on.

Her comment popped into my head a few years later when I visited F. W. de Klerk in the office of his foundation in Cape Town. He spoke proudly, presumably justifiably, of how his foundation was helping countries move along the road to peace and democracy; then he turned to another of his concerns. He was involved in efforts to ensure that the push for ethnic diversity did not give blacks an unfair advantage: "The question is, 'When would affirmative action cease to be affirmative action and become racism,'" he said. That he would be so worried about black advantage less than a decade after the end of apartheid gave more than a little credence to the businesswoman's concern.

Still, even if attention to historical wrongdoings tends to be fleeting, there is no denying the fact that efforts of the last few

decades to settle some historical accounts have yielded some powerful results. South Africa, Peru, and the other countries that have
so publicly wrestled with the demons of their past are no doubt
stronger democracies for having done so. The image of Swiss
banks, as attorney Michael Hausfeld pointed out, have likely been
altered forever. "No matter what, Swiss history will never be the
same," he said. There may even be, he believes, a lasting lesson
from their humiliation, namely an increased awareness that "there
is no neutrality when it comes to morality."

Whatever lesson one takes from that particular affair, the movement for recovered memory—for retroactive responsibility—is not
about to go away. We will continue to see groups demanding that
ancient wrongs be put right, that the current generation take
responsibility for not just the good but also the evil it has inherited.

"Where do you draw the line? How far back do you go? Do
you go back to Julius Caesar?" asked F. W. de Klerk in response to
a question I asked him about reparations. I suppose one goes as far
back as the unhealed wounds of the present require. For a nation,
that might mean looking back a few hundred years. For an adult
suffering from unresolved trauma, the time frame of the journey
would be considerably shorter.

Perhaps the more important question is not about time—and
how far back we should go—but about integrity: about how honest
we are prepared to be. It is the point made by Hugo van der Merwe
when I asked him about the primary mission of South Africa's
TRC: "It's about being honest and not telling ourselves lies."

For though it is certainly true, as noted above, that interpreta-
tions of events differ, that there will never be complete agreement
on history and its meaning, there are big truths that thinking people ought to be able to get right. What happened in Tulsa, for
instance, is not just a matter of opinion; there are facts, many of
them very ugly—and therefore, for some people, very difficult
to face.

Indeed, when it comes to history—personal or political—

facing unpleasant truths is always a challenge. It's somehow easier to cling to a reassuring lie. Hence the leader of a defeated Germany declared: "The overwhelming majority of the German people abhorred the crimes committed against the Jews and were not involved in them." No doubt others sincerely believe that the majority of white South Africans abhorred apartheid and that the majority of Turks abhorred violence against Armenians. If the majority was ever guilty of anything—the argument goes—it was simply accepting the deck that had been dealt. Yet the inconvenient and inescapable reality is that at some point, in virtually every case where atrocities took place, widespread acceptance became widespread approval.

In their respective books on the Tulsa massacre authors James Hirsch and Tim Madigan both comment on the historical makeover given Richard Lloyd Jones, the one-time owner of the *Tulsa Tribune,* the man whose racist editorializing was the match that ignited the mob's kerosene. Yet when Jones died, he was lauded as a great man. His involvement in the shameful incident was expunged from his record. Why? Because to acknowledge that he perpetrated so much evil would be an indictment not only of him but also of the community that so eagerly took him to its bosom.

In recent years, we have seen a host of convictions of Ku Klux Klan members whose crimes stretch back through the decades— of one who killed a black sharecropper, of another who killed four girls in a church, of yet another who murdered a civil rights leader, and the list goes on. Almost invariably they are portrayed as monsters unrepresentative of the good people all around them. Yet if they were monsters, why has it taken so long to bring them to justice? Why did their communities embrace them, shield them and refuse to convict them when they committed the crimes decades ago? If they were monsters, they were monsters with a lot of company. If they weren't exactly in the mainstream, they were close enough.

"All that is required for evil to prevail is for good men to do nothing," proclaimed Edmund Burke. At least he is credited with saying it. But it seems to me that Burke got it wrong. What is required is not that good men do nothing but that normal men embrace evildoers and sanction evil deeds; and because their hands are not dripping with blood, they insist they are good men. It seems to me that if we get nothing else from all this sifting through the past, we should at least get the fact that massive wrongdoing cannot take place without society's—sometimes silent—sanction.

Does facing up to such truths accomplish any real purpose? Does an honest accounting of history, at least the big truths of history, lead to hope for any meaningful type of reconciliation? Tutu obviously believes that it does: *To be able to forgive one needs to know whom one is forgiving and why. That is why the truth is so central to this whole exercise.* I can only hope Tutu is right. But even if Tutu is wrong, there is yet another reason to put aside the rosy glasses. With clearer vision, we will have a more realistic view of the problems the past has dumped in our laps—and we perhaps will also have a better sense of what we must do to solve them.

Whether we will, in fact, learn to view our respective societies more clearly is an open question. There may be something in human nature that makes us blind to much of the damage done in our name. But as information becomes more accessible, as the world becomes more wired, we may be surrendering a bit of our innocence. Wrongdoing on a grand scale is harder to hide than it once was—which means it is also harder to ignore.

In 2002, some months after East Timor celebrated its independence, I interviewed José Ramos-Horta, the Nobel Peace Prize laureate who serves as East Timor's minister of foreign affairs and cooperation. "The independence of East Timor is a by-product of the electronic age," he declared at one point. "In 1975, when we were invaded, there were far more killings. . . . And where was the world then? [The atrocities] did not make it into the prime time news of global television. There *was* no global television. . . .

There was no internet. The world had not been connected." When violence broke out in East Timor in 1999, he pointed out, "the world had changed. The media were everywhere. . . . That's what made Timor free. Without that, we would still be fighting— heroically, but still fighting."

His point was obvious—that the world today is not just a smaller place, it's also one in which we are less insulated than ever from the problems of people who once upon a time we might never have known.

A few months after my initial interviews, Amy—the woman sexually abused by her father—called with some exciting news. She had confronted her mother, yet again, over her mom ignoring the sexual assault on her daughter that had taken place before her eyes.

Initially, said Amy, her mother had done what she always does. She insisted that she had seen nothing and had known nothing; and that, anyway, it was the father who was at fault.

But Amy had refused to let her off the hook. "You need to understand how I felt a couple of years ago when we talked," Amy had told her; and she had explained how talking with her mother about that childhood incident always left her feeling betrayed and helpless all over again. Then she had asked a question: *Had Mom denied knowing for so long because she, herself, felt betrayed by her husband? Because she, herself, had had no idea what to say or what to do?*

The question drew a stunned silence from her mother and suddenly, reported Amy, "She broke down and bawled." Her mother admitted that she had indeed seen the abuse and she tearfully apologized.

Finally, she turned to Amy and asked what Amy would have her do.

"I told her, 'Let's just let it go. . . . Let's start today and create something new.' "

At last, she told me, she thought it was possible that she might build an "authentic" relationship with her mother. Finally, in acknowledging Amy's pain, and her own responsibility, her mother had made it possible for them to move forward. In accepting the burden of memory, in acknowledging a shameful secret she had tried to bury in the past, she had also, at least in Amy's view, taken a huge step toward self-awareness—toward sanctuary for a troubled soul.

Amy, of course, is just one person; and her story may have no universal lesson. It is, however, yet another illustration of the possibility of transformation, of the process of moving from deep denial to acceptance of responsibility and finally toward the promise of reconciliation. It is an illustration as well of the power of memory; and of how the ghosts of the past, if not properly buried, can continue to haunt the present.

All over the world, buried bones are being dug up—in Iraq, in Peru, in Rwanda, in Bosnia. And it is not just to turn the remains over to grieving families—though that is generally one of the purposes. There is also a growing awareness that those bones hold important information, information that can be of inestimable value to societies struggling to learn from their mistakes.

More often than not the answers are conditional and, in some respects, inconclusive. But the fact that the struggle goes on at all offers more than a glimmer of hope for a world that, in too many ways, has made a virtue out of ignorance and a gospel out of forgetting.

EPILOGUE

THE GHOST IN THE BUNKER, THE MAN IN THE HOLE

As THIS BOOK WENT TO PRESS AND PEOPLE embraced the spirit of the season of goodwill, a dirty, disheveled man climbed out of a hole in Iraq. It was almost as if, fifty-eight years ago, Adolf Hitler had emerged from the ruins of the Reich chancellery as something more vital than a corpse.

In taking his own life, Hitler relieved the Allies of responsibility for resolving his fate. Saddam Hussein was not so accommodating. He instead presented the world with the opportunity to put the fuehrer in the dock.

That Hussein would be tried, if caught alive, was never in doubt; the only questions were how and by whom—and whether any punishment could suffice for the crimes of which he would stand accused. Indeed, the argument over who would judge Hussein was in large part an argument over whether his execution would be an option on the table.

As debate raged, I found myself wondering about the point of it all. What purpose could any judicial proceeding conceivably serve when the alleged crimes were so immense and when the accused was a certified monster whom no one would grant the presumption of innocence? And what possible penalty could even begin to do justice?

Even death would be poor retribution. And, as Hamlet realized when contemplating Claudius's execution, death is not necessarily a punishment—but sometimes a favor. Perhaps Adolf Eichmann, the Nazi facilitator, went so bravely to his death because even before his capture his life—stripped of status and substantial material comfort—had become a form of hell.

In a sense, such ruminations were beside the point—as Allison Danner, an expert on international criminal tribunals at Vanderbilt University, pointed out. Hussein had been captured. *Something* had to be done. What was the alternative?

Of course, she was right. Something did have to be done. And tribunals are what civilized nations do. But aside from covering whatever punishment was ultimately meted out with a slight veneer of judicial impartiality, what would a tribunal accomplish? Why bother?

With crimes as "overwhelming, obvious and massive" as those committed by Hussein, justice was "beyond the scope of any actual judiciary," agreed Kenneth Anderson, a professor at American University's Washington College of Law. Winston Churchill had voiced much the same objection to the Nuremberg tribunal process, Anderson recalled.

Churchill reportedly favored executing most surviving Nazi leaders, as did U.S. Treasury Secretary Henry Morgenthau. But, in the end, advocates of an international tribunal prevailed. So between 1945 and 1949 the world watched an unprecedented spectacle as assorted Nazi leaders, some of whom were subsequently executed, were made to answer for the Holocaust.

The hope was that the Nuremberg trials would teach people, especially Germans, lessons—about the extent of the evil that had occurred and the unacceptability of going down that path ever again. Perhaps Hussein's trial also could teach. "Prove incredible events through credible evidence [and the] people in Iraq and throughout the world will understand the enormity of the atrocities," suggested Michael Scharf, director of the War Crimes Research Office at Case Western Reserve University and coauthor of *Peace with Justice? War Crimes and Accountability in the Former Yugoslavia*.

Yet, to the extent that postwar Germany is a model, the tribunal was not the best of teachers. German opinion shifted, but not always in a reliably progressive direction, and not necessarily in response to the Nuremberg proceedings. In an analysis published by South Africa's Centre for the Study of Violence and Reconciliation, Gunnar Theissen noted that during the very early phase of the Nuremberg trials, 53 percent of West Germans agreed that "National Socialism was in principle a good idea which was badly carried out." Months later, as the trials progressed and the reality of Nazi atrocities sank in, "agreement with this statement dropped to an average 40 percent," reported Theissen. But as more time passed, West Germans grew less critical of Nazism. By 1968, 55 percent thought Nazism was "a good idea badly carried out." Support for Hitler was also strong, and continued to be so for years thereafter. In 1975 some 38 percent of West Germans ranked Hitler among German's greatest statesmen—"if one disregarded the war."

As time passed, German attitudes changed radically. But that change, as Scharf acknowledged, followed show trials in Germany, a rewriting of German history books, passage of laws against Holocaust denial, and, perhaps most importantly, the dying out of the old and the coming of age of a new generation. Would Germans have progressed faster had Hitler himself been tried? Perhaps, though I suspect not.

In *Eichmann in Jerusalem,* Hannah Arendt observed that after the initial excitement, the audience for Eichmann's trial was not composed, for the most part, of those with much to learn: "It was filled with 'survivors,' with middle-aged and elderly people, immigrants from Europe, like myself, who knew by heart all there was to know, and who were in no mood to learn any lessons and certainly did not need this trial to draw their own conclusions." It was much the same observation offered by Nkosinathi Biko of South Africa's TRC proceedings: "a case of black people listening to their own story."

Show trials—as those of O.J. Simpson and Slobodan Milosevic alike make clear—are rarely good at forcing people to surrender strongly held beliefs. The villains in prosecutors' eyes are not necessarily villains in the eyes of members of the tribe. So you have Milosevic, Yugoslavia's former president and alleged war criminal, winning election to the Serbian parliament even as he is on trial in The Hague.

No judgment of Hussein is likely to convince anyone who is not already convinced that he is a greater evil than his captors or that Iraqi Bathism is worse than American imperialism. And regardless of what facts come to light, if the experiences of assorted tribunals and truth commissions are a guide, it will not bring about closure or heal a hurting nation. At best, it will jumpstart the process.

So, again: Why bother? Well, as Professor Danner observed, that is what civilized societies do when the accused is in the stockade. Answers must be demanded—particularly if it is the fuehrer himself, as opposed to just his henchmen, who waits in the dungeon—even if we know in advance that the answers given will not be satisfactory. There are also, of course, pragmatic, even cynical, political reasons—the need to thoroughly discredit the prior regime, or to *ex post facto* justify an inadequately justified war. But there is another reason as well, one perhaps related to the disposition to believe in the unseen and unverifiable Divine. It has to do with the human need for hope and the consequent capacity for faith.

Though the man in the dock is the focus of the process, in reality it is not so much about him. How could it be when everyone

pretty much knows the outcome before it begins? It is about values, and the need to reaffirm them. And it is about a people, or
peoples, trying to convince themselves that there is progress in the
world, that we can, indeed, learn from the past; that we are better
than the devils we often choose to lead us. And it is finally about a
responsibility to a generation yet unborn to make a bit of sense of
the world we leave behind.

Ellis Cose

BIBLIOGRAPHY

Arendt, Hannah. *Eichmann in Jerusalem* (New York: Viking Press, 1963; New York: Penguin Books, 1994).

Authers, John, and Richard Wolffe. *The Victim's Fortune* (New York: HarperCollins, 2002).

Barkan, Elazar. *The Guilt of Nations* (Baltimore and London: The Johns Hopkins University Press, 2000).

Bazyler, Michael J. "The Holocaust Movement in Comparative Perspective," *Berkeley Journal of International Law,* vol. 20, no. 1, 2002.

Blumenfeld, Laura. *Revenge* (New York, London, Toronto: Washington Square Press, 2003).

Boraine, Alex. *A Country Unmasked* (New York, Oxford, Cape Town: Oxford University Press, 2000).

de Kock, Eugene, and Jeremy Gordin. *A long night's DAMAGE* (Saxonwold, South Africa: Contra Press, 1998).

Denis, Philippe. *Orality, Memory & the Past* (Pietermaritzburg, South Africa: Cluster Publications, 2000).

Eizenstat, Stuart E. *Imperfect Justice* (New York: Public Affairs, 2003).

Enright, Robert D. *Forgiveness Is a Choice* (Washington: American Psychological Association, 2001).

Enright, Robert D., and Richard F. Fitzgibbons. *Helping Clients Forgive* (Washington: American Psychological Association, 2002).

Enright, Robert D., and Joanna North, eds. *Exploring Forgiveness* (Madison, Wisconsin: The University of Wisconsin Press, 1998).

Erikson, Kai. *A New Species of Trouble* (New York, London: W. W. Norton, 1994).

Gobodo-Madikizela, Pumla. *A Human Being Died That Night* (Boston, New York: Houghton Mifflin Company, 2003).

Gorringe, Timothy. *God's Just Vengeance* (Cambridge: Cambridge University Press, 1996).

Graybill, Lyn S. *Religion and Resistance Politics in South Africa* (Westport, Conn.: Praeger, 1995).

Hayner, Priscilla B. *Unspeakable Truths* (New York, Routledge, 2001).

Helmick, Raymond G., S. J., and Rodney Petersen, eds. *Forgiveness and Reconciliation* (Radnor, Penn.: Temple Foundation Press, 2001).

Hirsch, James S. *Riot and Remembrance* (Boston, New York: Houghton Mifflin Company, 2002).

Khamisa, Azim. *From Murder to Forgiveness* (La Jolla: ANK Publishing, 1998).

King Jr., Martin Luther. *A Testament of Hope* (New York: HarperCollins, 1986).

Kluger, Ruth. *Still Alive* (New York: The Feminist Press at the City University of New York, 2001).

Lamb, Sharon, and Jeffrie G. Murphy, eds. *Before Forgiving* (Oxford, New York: Oxford University Press, 2002).

Langholtz, Harvey J, ed. *The Psychology of Peacekeeping* (Westport, Conn.: Praeger, 1998).

Madigan, Tim. *The Burning* (New York: St. Martin's Press, 2001).

Maki, Mitchell T., Harr H. L. Kitano, and Meagan Berthold. *Achieving the Impossible Dream* (Urbana and Chicago: University of Illinois Press, 1999).

Marongiu, Pietro, and Graeme Newman. *Vengeance* (Totowa, New Jersey: Rowman & Littlefield, 1987).

Massaquoi, Hans J. *Destined to Witness* (New York: William Morrow and Company, 1999).

McCullough, Michael E., C. Garth Bellah, Shelley Dean Kilpatrick, Judith L. Johnson. "Vengefulness: Relationships with Forgiveness, Rumination, Well-Being, and the Big Five," *Personality and Social Psychology Bulletin,* vol. 27, no. 5., May 2001.

Minow, Martha, ed. *Breaking the Cycles of Hatred* (Princeton and Oxford: Princeton University Press, 2002).

Murphy, Jeffrie G. *Getting Even* (Oxford, New York: Oxford University Press, 2003).

Neuborne, Burt. "Holocaust Reparations Litigation: Lessons for the Slavery Reparations Movement," *New York University Annual Survey of American law,* vol. 58., 2003.

Ntsimane, Radikobo. "A Mirage Called Forgiveness: A Critique of the Truth and Reconciliation Commission," in *Orality Memory and the Past,* edited by Philippe Denis (Pietermaritzburg, South Africa: Cluster Publications, 2000).

Oklahoma Commission to Study the Tulsa Race Riot of 1921, *Tulsa Race Riot* (State of Oklahoma, 2001).

Oliver, Melvin L., and Thomas M. Shapiro. *Black Wealth/White Wealth* (New York, London: Routledge, 1997).

Pauw, Jacques. *Into the Heart of Darkness* (Jeppestown, South Africa: Jonathan Ball Publishers Ltd., 1997).

Pross, Christian. *Paying for the Past* (Baltimore, London: The Johns Hopkins University Press, 1998).

Robinson, Randall. *The Debt* (New York: E. P. Dutton, 2000).

Sarat, Austin. *When the State Kills* (Princeton, Oxford: Princeton University Press, 2001).

Schimmel, Solomon. *Wounds Not Healed by Time* (Oxford, New York: Oxford University Press, 2002).

Schlink, Bernard. *The Reader* (New York: Pantheon Books, trans. copyright 1997, original 1995).

Staub, Ervin. *The Roots of Evil* (Cambridge, New York: Cambridge University Press, 1989).

Theissen, Gunnar. *Between acknowledgement and ignorance: How white South Africans have dealt with the aparthied past* (Johannesburg: Centre for the Study of Violence and Reconciliation, 1997).

Turow, Scott. *Ultimate Punishment* (New York: Farrar, Straus & Giroux, 2003).

Weisenthal, Simon. *The Sunflower,* 2nd ed. (New York: Schocken Books, 1997).

Winbush, Raymond A. ed. *Should America Pay?* (New York: HarperCollins, 2003).

INDEX